We Talk, We Lead:

A REFLECTION OF ONE WOMAN'S STORIES
TO INSPIRE AND EMPOWER OTHERS

WENDY ZELOND

Ruth,
Thank you for your support
and encouragement. Let's
start conversations, because
when we talk, we lead.
keep smiling.
Wendy

ISBN: 1986930408
ISBN-13: 978-1986930406

DEDICATION

To Matt and Graeme,
I love you both no matter what.

CONTENTS

INTRODUCTION

I often get asked, what is my secret? How did I achieve corporate success — at a young age and as a woman, no less? How did I make it look so easy, and what did I have to sacrifice to gain it? Much to the dismay of the information seeker, I usually shrug my shoulders, tilt my head, and downplay my achievements while quickly changing the subject away from myself.

Now, before you get excited and start picking apart my behavior (because, yes, I *do* see the problem with my lack of response), let me tell you a little bit more about myself and my journey.

My name is Wendy, the girl next door, raised in the small town of Katy, Texas. I loved playing sports — tennis was my game of choice — enjoying Friday night lights, and hanging out with friends. I was a good student, but not top of class. I was the quintessential middle child in an upper-middle-class home. We ate family dinners almost every night, and my parents are still together. I did not want for anything, but also did not think I was owed anything. I knew that I was expected to go to college and get a job when I graduated. And that's exactly what I did.

Fast-forward 15 years, three industries and one international move (OK, it was Canada, but it still counts), I found myself promoted to an executive position at a Fortune 500 company in my 30s. I did not achieve this corporate success by following what others might call the customary route. I don't have a perfect resume. I started college thinking I would take advantage of my years as a tennis player and major in physical education, but after an advisor encouraged me to take an accounting course, I was hooked. I graduated with an accounting degree and was hired by a Big Five firm right out of school. And even though I struggled to pass the CPA exam, I loved public accounting. Sadly, I had to transition out of it before I was ready. I took a demotion to go to work for a publicly held energy company and started the climb again, which included obtaining my MBA and having my first child, in no particular order. And then — at age 36 — I became the Chief Financial Officer for a major business unit and started managing more than 120 people.

I have a husband who provides immense support, a son I miss when late nights and travel keep me away, and a big, big job. I also have a heck of a lot of fun at work.

So I do understand why people ask how I got here, and I do understand that it is time for me to stop downplaying my achievements and maybe even share a secret or two.

It is time for me to join the conversation. No, wait, it's time for me to lead a conversation.

Here's the thing: if not for the women in my life and in my corporate world — who've listened to me, lent a shoulder as well as an ear, and counseled me with their wise voices — I'd probably be a far less successful version of myself.

Throughout my journey, we shared stories and made true, honest connections, discussing topics that are still on women's minds today. Topics like:

- Balancing home and family with life at the office...and making sure nothing and no one gets short shrift.

- How to advance in a (still) male-dominated work world.

- Finding a mentor who will genuinely advocate for you — and being a mentor for others.

As I've moved from company to company and up the corporate ladder, I've found that women may not feel comfortable talking about issues like these with each other. Maybe we're afraid of exposing a weakness or worry we won't look as confident as we're supposed to, day-after-business-day. Or perhaps trust is an issue: when we see each other more as competitors than colleagues, we might be reluctant to share something we fear can be used against us.

And even when we have the desire to talk about the tough issues, it's not always easy to get the conversation started or to truly support one another. Overcoming those barriers is where I want to help.

In this book, you'll find short stories that depict what my journey has been like. They don't just apply to executives — I talk about things that women at all levels can relate to, including:

- Being open to possibilities — there is more than one path to get you where you want to go.

- How to avoid carrying baggage from your past that could hinder your future.

- Salary negotiations — why women traditionally aren't good at them, how we can improve, and how to get what we're worth.

- How missteps are just as important as triumphs when you allow them to strengthen you.

Each story takes five minutes or less to read (when you're juggling work, family, and all of the other interests in your life, five minutes may be all the time you have to spare!). In each one, you'll find questions you can ask among colleagues and friends to get the conversation going...and keep it rolling. You may find you have more in common than you think.

Sharing thoughts, experiences, and even setbacks could be just what you need to help you grow and flourish in your career...because when *We Talk, We Lead.*

Wendy's Way to Success: The Iced Tea Trick

As a gregarious person, I don't have much trouble talking — to anyone. But I know that it's not always easy to lean around the cubicle wall and ask, "Hey, have time to visit?"

I've got a trick for getting people to talk, and it relies on iced tea.

I'm a native Texan. And if iced tea isn't the official state drink, it should be. Don't be fooled by Coke or that other Lone Star treasure, Dr Pepper. There is nothing as delicious and refreshing as a tall glass of iced tea. Just thinking about the black currant iced tea I drank during my last visit to Houston makes me thirsty and filled with longing ...

You get the point: I'm just a little addicted. I can't make it through the day without an iced-tea fix (or several, but who's counting?).

Now, someone else might have their administrative assistant go down the hall, make some iced tea, and bring it back to them, but I prefer to go to the kitchen and brew it myself.

That's not because I have unmatched tea-making skills or I'm super fussy. It's just that as I walk through my department and down to the kitchen, I pick up people along the way. We have impromptu conversations and informal problem-solving sessions. I can be a sounding board, and I get feedback I might not hear in a more structured setting.

And yes, sometimes we just chat and get to know one another better. These little journeys take anywhere from two minutes to 20. And even though we're basically taking a break, we're totally engaged with one another.

Try it sometime. You will be surprised how personable and productive you can be standing next to a tall glass of iced tea (or whatever your beverage choice)!

Learning to
Let Go

We Talk, We Lead

CHAPTER 1: LEARNING TO LET GO

For most people, letting go of established ways of thinking and established patterns of behavior isn't easy: we often equate letting go to losing control.

But to grow in our jobs and become better leaders, changing our outlook and the way we deal with people and situations is not just a good idea — it's often required. We may even have to let go of long-held dreams, like having a certain title or working in a specific environment.

When I started my career, I brought the competitive attitude I'd forged as a student athlete into the workplace. Accustomed as a singles tennis player to being solely responsible for my success, I micromanaged the people who worked with me. I thought the best way to accomplish our goals was my *way; I didn't want to fail because I relied on someone else who might "mess up." I was, of course, neglecting the fact that other people have talents and can make contributions... and those contributions might be a lot better than what I could have come up with. In my heart, I knew there wasn't just one way of doing things, but I had to get my brain to believe it.*

Then I had a wake-up call, or rather, a wake-up email in the middle of the night.

It seemed I was following in my boss's oppressive footsteps — and I didn't particularly like the way that path looked. I realized that my mindset was holding me back and weighing me down.

As a result, I changed my ways. No, it wasn't easy. And it took time. But my new way of working made me the kind of leader people want to work with and for. Sure, not everything I do is greeted with applause; part of my continuing growth is learning to let go of criticism — and taking the compliments with a grain of salt, too. I've also discovered that if something goes wrong, there's a way to take responsibility, gracefully.

Taking the Spotlight off Myself and Shining It on Others

A good leader takes a little more than his share of the blame, a little less than his share of the credit[1] *– Arnold H. Glasgow, businessman and author*

Whether you are just starting out or well into your career, it's nice to be recognized for the hard work you do. Who doesn't like a pat on the back, sincere thanks, or a bonus in the form of a gift, some time off, or a little extra cash in the paycheck?

I have discovered, though, that certain leaders are more likely to *take* credit than to hand it out, stealing the recognition that their team members deserve.

Has that ever happened to you? You've done most of the heavy lifting, but your boss basked in the glory of **your** job well done? It's infuriating and unfair. And, it can diminish trust — which is critical to positive relationships and the long-term success of a team.

As career coach Chrissy Scivicque writes in an ivyexec.com blog post, when a manager takes the credit that belongs to others, team members see it as a betrayal. They'll question the manager's motives and worry that they're secretly being held down.[2]

Granted, some people are naturally better at divvying up credit than others. Depending on your personality, it can be a tall order to put into action Mr. Glasgow's advice, above. That doesn't mean it can't be done.

And if I can do it, so can you. Sharing the spotlight didn't come naturally to me but was a lesson I learned along the way.

As a varsity tennis player in college, primarily playing singles, I generally had only myself to depend on for the win. When I won, the applause was all mine and boy, that felt good. I'll be honest: I was happy **not** sharing the thrill of victory. I grew accustomed to being the focus of attention, which made me even more competitive and driven to succeed.

My coach, who would have been justified in being recognized for my achievements, understood how motivating praise can be. He recognized how hard I'd practiced and how tough I played and let me have center stage for myself. Never once did he come running onto the court to say, "Look what I did! I made her the baseliner she is today! This is as much my victory as it is hers!"

He could have, but he didn't. And the fact that he didn't feel compelled to talk about his contribution was a pretty important lesson for me, although I did not realize it until some years later.

As you can imagine, I brought an athlete's competitive fervor to the work world. And while I was achieving great results, I was willing to step on anyone in my way to achieve my goals. I micromanaged, nit-picked, and thought no project could succeed unless it had my touch. I might never have changed if I hadn't gone to work for someone with similar traits.

Obviously, when I took the position there was no way to know exactly what this person would be like as a boss. I was just happy and excited to be working for a woman who had become an executive, and who — I thought — would model behaviors that would help me become a leader, too.

Unfortunately, it wasn't long before I realized what a nightmare she could be. Yes, you heard me: a dark, persistent *nightmare.* Suddenly, I had first-hand knowledge of how difficult it is to be managed by someone who scrutinizes every detail of your work, refuses to share credit, and who behaves in a passive-aggressive manner. You know, like emailing me at 2 a.m. to see if I was awake and working, then following up two hours later — still well before any sensible person would be fully functional, if you ask me — with a note that says, "I thought I could count on you but I guess I was wrong."

Not only that, she was condescending and patronizing and, the more I thought about the characteristics I didn't like about her, the more I saw some of the same ones in myself. I was mortified. Watching this woman at work was like looking at a mirror into the future. If I didn't change my ways, I would see her face in my reflection. I didn't like that outlook at all. And I certainly didn't want to be responsible for someone else ever feeling the way I did at that moment.

I saw myself in my nit-picking, controlling, credit-hogging boss and vowed to change. There's enough praise to go around — I could heap it on my team members without feeling my own contributions were being ignored. Did you know that recognizing others is actually one way of getting your own accomplishments noticed? Here's how that works: when you say something like, "Joan did X, Mary did Y, and I did Z," you thank others while promoting yourself. You've included your own role without coming off as a preening narcissist.

So, I thought back to the positive influence my college coach had been and decided to adopt his style. I moved from tearing people down to building them up. Where a conversation in the past might have started with me asking, "Why did you do it like that?" instead I learned to say, "That's great output, but it could be stronger if we did this." And although it took some time, I dialed down my need for admiration and acclaim. Now, my team members get the credit because they've done the work, simple as that. I might have a stellar idea, but it's my team who makes it a reality. My job as a leader is to create spaces where people can succeed. When they do, **they** should be recognized for it, not me.

And you know what? I found out that remaining humble and turning the attention toward my team members actually feels pretty darned good, too. I've also learned that there is enough praise to go around; that no one's work — even my own — has to go unnoticed. Handing out recognition to my team doesn't mean I won't be acknowledged or appreciated by those around me.

Now, I don't use recognition just to reinforce good behavior. I'm no Pavlov, and my team members aren't trained to expect a reward for their every action. But as I've progressed upward in the corporate world, I realized I have a different vantage point and therefore better perspective on what's around me. Some people think the higher they go, the more they are able do everything themselves. As for me, I've realized that some members of our team can achieve things I'd never be able to do, and others have certain skills that far surpass my own. They really *are* worthy of the spotlight.

Conversation Starters

Here are some suggestions to spark conversation in your own circles and explore your personal experiences:

How have you let go of attitudes or behaviors to be the kind of team member or leader you wanted to be?

You've been overshadowed by a glory seeker — what did you do?

The Good, the Bad, and the In-Between. Why I Tune It All Out.

"You're a breath of fresh air."

"Bet you only got the job because you're a woman."

"You're our favorite."

"Why do you always talk so loud?"

"You are the only woman I have liked working for."

"Aren't you too young for this job?"

That dueling banjos-style commentary represents a few of the actual compliments and criticisms I've received.

Clearly, some people are my fans. Others, not so much. That's OK. To me, what matters more than tallying my admirers and detractors is how I handle the comments I hear about myself and my work, whether they're nice or not.

I'm not talking about the performance management process or the insight my mentors share with me. That's essential, open and honest feedback aimed at helping me improve my work — and I will be the first to say I appreciate every bit of it as I continue learning, growing, and developing.

I'm referring to flowery commendations and gut-punching disapprovals, and how I react to either.

I understand that the way each of us responds to compliments and complaints is highly individual. Some of us are good at clinging to the favorable remarks and brushing off the less-positive observations. Some of us reject any whiff of praise, but replay hurtful statements over and over.

You know what works for me? Letting go of all of it: the good, the bad, and the in-between.

That doesn't mean I don't enjoy praise. It's nice to hear things like, "You're the best leader we've ever had."

But I've learned you just can't take either admiration or reproach to heart.

Let me explain. My bias is toward action and achievement, whether anyone notices and comments, or not. I am a high energy, highly motivated person, and those qualities are amplified by the people around me. And as you've heard, I'm a wee bit competitive. If I see you putting in 100 percent, I'll match you and more. Compliments — anything that seems to be "all talk," in fact — won't make me work harder than I already do.

And what about criticism? I see no value in listening to derogatory messages. I can't allow insults to diminish my confidence that I'm doing what's right in the long term.

(Plus, let's face it: no matter where you work, you're bound to come across people who are just downbeat, discouraging, or nasty. No matter what you do, they'll find fault. If you recognize that someone is chronically giving the thumbs down, their opinion probably isn't valid, anyway.)

I know that it's not always easy to tune out the nay-sayers. One of the greatest challenges we face in the workplace is knowing how to respond to negative or abusive remarks. So, what is the best course when someone attacks or insults us?

As your kindergarten teacher probably told you, it's best to do nothing. That's right. Don't argue. Don't mount your own offensive attack. When you're silent, it prevents the situation from escalating.

Oh, I realize how hard it can be to keep quiet. For some people, there is nothing as satisfying as a sharp rejoinder to the person who has upset them. Studies have shown that even the nicest person can become aggressive and mean under certain circumstances.

But to keep things productive — I mean, you'll probably still have to work with your provoker tomorrow — it's best to keep things civil and to let your cooler head prevail.

Consider what happened when a person asked me, point blank, if I actually do any work.

That's a pretty serious attack, and it definitely irked me. But instead of launching a counteroffensive, asking how much work he did, or telling him to look at the results I've achieved, all I said was, "I hope that as you get to know me and my work ethic, you won't have to ask that anymore." (Sure, sometimes it's tougher to dismiss a remark or judge-y observation. When I'm struggling to let it go, I find a trusted confidant who will lend an ear — or go with me to grab a Blizzard.)

While that question was about my commitment and competence, I know women hear more insults and negative comments about their appearance than anything else. Look at how often the media rakes female celebrities over the coals about their clothing choices, hairstyles, or going out in public without a full face of makeup. Women are regularly judged for their bodies — too curvy, not attractive enough, too wrinkly or pimply, you name it. (In one of the greatest ironic slams of all time, Mindy Lahiri, creator and star of television's *The Mindy Project*, was once told that **she wasn't pretty enough to play herself.**)[3]

Sadly, I've gotten my share of scrutiny over my looks, too. More than once, I've been told I don't look like an executive — although I imagine that, like beauty, executive appearance is in the eye of the beholder. I'll admit I'm a little on the chubby side, and that I probably look even younger than I am. I make a conscious effort to put on a little makeup every day and I dress professionally (except when it's Ugly Sweater Day), thanks to the help I get from a personal shopper at Nordstrom, who taught me to ignore size labels and get things that fit and make me feel good about myself. (That was a real confidence-booster, by the way. Yes, some people question why I need help with my wardrobe, but here's what I tell them: I can't cut my own hair, and no one thinks anything of me going to a hair salon. Why should it be any different with my clothes or any other aspect of my appearance?)

Truthfully, though, I'm not sure how any of this affects my work or why it should be anyone's concern. Conversation about my appearance isn't meaningful or valuable; I don't come to work to be ogled, and my choice to wear pants or a skirt on any given day doesn't determine my productivity. So when I hear a comment about my looks or fashion sense, there's just no point in me responding or letting it affect my confidence.

Sure, compliments are nice to hear. And although I don't need them to keep me moving forward, you might find them highly motivating. The toxic remarks can be a little trickier to deal with. I know they're hard to turn a deaf ear to, and it's easy to want to attack in response. But that only gives the provoker the satisfaction of knowing they've gotten under your skin. What's worked for me is to keep calm and respond in a sensible, mature way. No name-calling, no threats of retribution: just the facts.

Letting go of the compliments and criticisms takes willpower — and practice. But I've found it's worth the extra effort. It's one of the reasons I can stay honest with myself and my team, feel confident that we're going forward, and generally be positive. Concentrating on my own internal voice, and discarding the distractions, helps me be the leader I want to be.

Conversation Starters

How important is it to you to hear praise about your performance? Does it motivate you?

What's the best response to criticism that you've ever made...or heard? What made that response particularly effective?

Release the Hurt, Remember the Lesson

Although I'm experienced at downplaying both compliments and criticism, I'll admit that a few comments have been tougher than others to shake off or put into perspective. Eventually, I've been able to overcome them, but it has taken a little more time or effort. Why? The reason typically relates to who made the remark. I think we'd all agree that the unkind words of someone we care about or trust can sting us more than others.

For example, although I've made peace with it, I don't know if I'll ever forget the time Chris, my former boss — a great, outgoing guy who was one of my favorite people — told me **he hated me** for helping another employee.

No, he wasn't trying to be ironic or funny. He was upset with me, and he chose hurtful language to express it.

We had worked so well together. We had a wonderful relationship. We even had the same birthday. How did we get to the point where he could say that he hated me?

11

I mean, I know how we got here. I had recently moved to another division and a woman from his department — let's call her Kathy — came to work for me. Her reasons for wanting the transfer were pretty easy for anyone to understand: I could offer her a position with a higher salary and a flexible work schedule.

The only problem was, inevitably, the people back in Chris's department found out about Kathy's new arrangement. And, you guessed it: they wanted adjustments to their wages as well. That made Chris angry to the point that it ended our friendship.

The fact that my actions ultimately benefited a larger group of people could be traced back to me with a dotted line, I suppose, but that wasn't my original intent. It's just the way things sometimes unfold in business.

Over time, I've been able to sort out why this affected Chris to the point that he could effectively obliterate our relationship with a few, choice words.

It hurt like hell to be told by my former boss that he hated me for helping another woman get the salary she deserved. But the experience made me a better leader and more willing to take responsibility when things didn't go well. Notice that I said responsibility, not blame. Chris was blaming me — using that childlike instinct to say "not me," and finding someone else to make liable. Sure, no one likes to be "at fault," but we all make mistakes. Whether you call it accepting responsibility or being accountable — or just behaving like an adult — working to understand what went wrong and developing ways to prevent it from happening again are key characteristics of good leadership.

I imagine he considered my actions a personal affront — as if I had torn up some imaginary contract between the two of us.

I'm sorry he felt that way. But I'm not responsible for anything more than giving a team member a part-time job at the wage she deserved.

The incident got me thinking, though: why does it bother us more when we're criticized or insulted by someone who we've gotten along well with?

Tris Thorp, lifestyle and leadership coach, explains: in every relationship, workplace or otherwise, we have established boundaries. Typically, we recognize those boundaries in various ways — by respecting one another's opinions, even when we disagree with them; by not pointing out each other's faults; and/or by being happy when the other person succeeds. When someone oversteps those boundaries, it's startling and shocking.[4]

And it hurts like hell.

I can't imagine too many people laughing off a comment like, "I hate you."

But, I've been able to file it away. Recalling it isn't the same as being upset by it. And, to be honest, I learned a lot from the entire incident, especially about going against the grain in a corporate environment. If I'd communicated better with Chris — given him advance notice about the offer I was going to make to Kathy, for example — our relationship might have remained intact. Or he might still have been angry. His feelings wouldn't have kept me from doing what I thought was fair for her.

I also learned that, as a leader, I need to take responsibility when something doesn't go my way or has an unpleasant outcome. I don't want to be like Chris, who blamed me for having to give raises, when the problem could have been avoided by him paying them what they were worth.

When I think of Chris's remark, I no longer dwell on the hurt. Instead, I remember the lessons.

Conversation Starters

Have you experienced a negative work situation that turned into a lesson for you? If you could go back and change things, what would you do differently?

Have you ever been the scapegoat for a problem or conflict at work? How did that turn out?

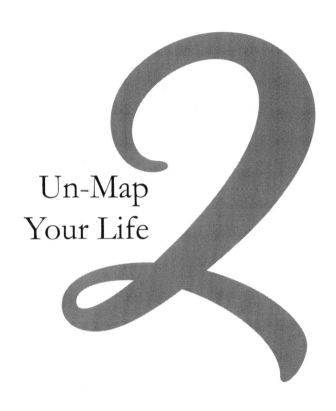

Un-Map
Your Life

We Talk, We Lead

CHAPTER 2: UN-MAP YOUR LIFE

In my experience, most successful women are planners. We know what we want and we have thought about (maybe even written down) the steps it will take to get us where we want to go.

The only thing is: we're not in this journey alone. Sometimes, we get cut off, or the way is filled with roadblocks and potholes. Other times, your own personal GPS helps you find the short cuts and make all the green lights.

My advice? Leave enough flexibility in your plan for the unexpected.

You just have to face that things will be out of your control. What's important is how you respond when that happens. Will you panic? Shut down? Or get on with your life, even though circumstances aren't ideal? The path you ultimately wind up on might not be the one you imagined, but that doesn't mean it's wrong or bad. Great disappointments can lead to great things.

So apply for the job you think you'd love and excel at, even if you don't meet every qualification in the ad. Turn down the promotion if your gut says it's not right. Keep your options open and have faith in your instincts. Did you know that intuition — that funny feeling you get about something — has a scientific basis? And that women are better at making a successful decision based on intuition than men are?[5] If I hadn't trusted a sinking sensation about a long-desired European move, I might have wound up high and dry in Luxembourg, which would not have been as romantic as it may sound. Or I might have agreed to live with a small-time drug-dealer — that wouldn't have looked great on my resume.

Good Opportunity, Bad Timing:
The Wisdom to Walk Away

Occasionally, we base our hopes for the future on a single idea that we think would make our lives perfect — or pretty close, anyhow. But, in some cases, that narrow focus actually imposes limits on us. It's only when we shake free of it that we can really find happiness.

For example, when I was in my early 20s beginning my career, I had an overwhelming desire to make my mark somewhere — *anywhere* — other than my hometown of Houston.

If opportunity can be as close as your backyard or as far as a remote pinpoint on the map, my choice was to go the distance. Moving up was a goal, sure. But moving *away* was a priority.

I had returned to Houston after college with a newly minted business degree and a job with a Big Five accounting firm. I understood that my life was the kind many other new grads would covet.

Yet, landing back home seemed too much like starting back at square one. How could I stretch my wings if they might bump into Mom and Dad?

So, when my firm's Luxembourg office announced it was looking for someone with my auditing experience, it took me all of about a half-second to decide to apply. Imagine, doing the work I loved, only in Europe instead of downtown Houston. I couldn't have dreamed of a more exciting opportunity.

I flew to Luxembourg for an interview. During my whirlwind trip, I toured the office, met the senior manager I'd be working with — great guy, loved him — visited my future apartment, and signed an offer letter.

I was on my way.

Except then I wasn't.

This was late summer 2001. I had started to pack and my going-away party was penciled in on my calendar. But then came the terrible events of September 11.

Obviously, the tragedies of that day eclipsed everyone's plans. Like the airlines, I, too, was put on ground-hold. The world had changed so much since I'd signed the offer. Was this a good time to make a life-altering move? I had decided I needed a few weeks to think things over, to see if the world calmed down, when one of the senior partners called me into his office.

The Luxembourg job was still mine, he said, but I shouldn't be afraid to speak up if I no longer wanted to go.

The fact was, my instincts (my 'gut') were telling me I should stay put.

It was devastating to pull the plug on my European ambition, but the decision actually saved me a great deal of turmoil down the road. Because soon after I made the decision to stay, the fortunes of the public accounting firm I worked for started to unravel. Because of work visa complications on their end, if I had moved to Europe, I would have been without a job or a paid way home.

Of course, I was relieved that things had worked out in my favor, but I still didn't want to be stranded in Houston, either.

Sadly, the troubles of our public accounting firm were only getting worse. Our jobs were no longer secure. So even though I still loved public accounting, I decided my wanderlust might be better served if I worked in the travel industry. I started interviewing with airlines, and one of them thought I'd be the ideal candidate for an internal auditing position open in Washington, D.C.

OK, it's not Europe. But Washington, D.C. is a lot more than a stone's throw away from my parents' place. My favorite cousin lived there, and as a bit of a political junkie, I loved the idea of being in the national hub. So off I went to D.C. for a round of interviews. Again, I entered the situation believing it would be perfect for me. And, again, I was wrong. Really wrong.

My first warning signal was when one of the experienced auditors told me, off the record, that the company wasn't a good place to work. My interview with the department head confirmed it — he said things about his team members that were so appalling, I almost got up and walked out. But in the back of my mind, I saw this job as a stepping stone, not a lifetime commitment. I stayed in my seat.

I almost sacrificed my values for a job because it met the criteria of being far from home. In the long run, I discovered that you can't force things to fit your fantasies. The right place might be right under your nose. My instincts told me to stay, which begs the question: should you trust your gut when it comes to making a business or career decision? After all, you usually have a lot of hard evidence in front of you and that might seem sufficient. Psychology, however, suggests that even in the face of all the facts, sometimes it's best to act on your hunches (and, incidentally, women are a lot more instinctual than men). Whether you've used nothing but reason or added some intuition to the decision-making process, the most important thing is to accept that, for now, you have made the best possible choice. Don't try to second-guess yourself.

Over dinner with my cousin that evening, I told her about my potential boss and his revolting comment. I never want to be a leader like that, I said, but for the sake of the job and the location, I'd make accommodations and go to work for him.

This should have tipped me off to the fact that I might have been sidestepping my personal principles a bit. Instead, it took one more forehead-smacking incident for me to reach that point.

With housing prices in D.C. best described as astronomical, I realized it was unlikely I'd be able to live alone. A friend of a friend was looking for a roommate, and I agreed to meet him.

We drove to his townhouse in one of D.C.'s trendy neighborhoods, the kind of area where you could walk your dog or walk to a bar. The place looked nice enough — two-story brick with black shutters. Yes, please, I thought.

But one step inside and my nose curled. What in heaven's name was that earthy, herby, sort-of-skunky smell? I looked questioningly at my prospective roommate who shrugged, smirked slightly, and said, "I sense you're cool — do you have an issue with pot?"

"Well, I don't smoke it," I answered, "but… "

Turned out, the person grew pot in his attic. "Oh, but don't worry," he said. "I don't sell it out of the house."

And I was thinking, "Fine. I'll live here. This is the perfect set-up. Airline… audit… cousin… roommate… even if I'll be working for a jerk and pot is growing over my head…"

Finally, it hit me: am I really willing to sacrifice my values for this job?

The answer, of course, was *no*. Remaining true to myself was essential. *Who* I am is always more important than *where* I am.

So back to Houston I went. But, you know, things turned out pretty well. Within a month, I was hired by a major airline based there.

And two years later, I met my husband. If I'd gone to Europe or D.C., or anywhere else for that matter, the most important relationship of my life would never have happened, and neither would the son I adore.

Yes, I let go of my dream to move (although eventually I relocated to Canada after joining the energy industry). I realized that rather than accepting what was right in front of me, I was trying to force things to fit my fantasies. When I finally embraced my present and stopped clinging to that single idea — that being in Houston was limiting me — I actually found how limitless my future could be.

Conversation Starters

Where are you willing to compromise or leave room for the unexpected?

Have you ever made a decision that contradicted what your instincts were telling you? What were the results?

How does your current position mesh with your "dream job?" What do you value most about this stage of your career?

You Are Not the Decider

I remember back in 2006, when President George W. Bush was mocked mercilessly for calling himself "the decider" when asked if then-Secretary of Defense, Donald Rumsfeld, should remain on his team.

"I'm the decider, and I decide what's best,[6]" the President said.

His critics jumped on what they considered his poor command of the

21

English language. Comedy shows like *Saturday Night Live* had a field day with his slip-up, and the term decider even made it into the Urban Dictionary, where it is defined as "the supreme ultimate decision maker in the world.[7]"

Not only did the fallout from the President's comment amuse us, it provided an important lesson: be thoughtful about your word choices, unless you want to wind up the butt of a running joke (although being made fun of on SNL might actually be kind of cool).

But there is some truth in his faux pas and that is this: when it comes to that next position or promotion, **someone other than you** — like a hiring manager or executive — is largely the decider. So don't think that dream job is out of reach if you don't exactly match all of the requirements.

I say this because, over and over, I've seen women disqualify themselves from applying for jobs they would probably be good at and love.

Why do we do this? Are we protecting ourselves from disappointment or rejection? Is it because job-hunting is a competition, and we feel that we have to be at the top of our game to even begin to play? Sometimes, women hold themselves back because they don't want to disappoint or upset their co-workers, who have come to depend upon them and might have to pick up the slack if they leave. Or they fear the department might not be able to handle the change if they leave. That, of course, is not your problem to worry about. And, really, no one is indispensable.

If your education and experience do not exactly match what the employer is looking for, but you have the desire within you to prove that this is YOUR job, you have nothing to lose by applying. I will take a prospective team member who has a deep, gut-wrenching desire to prove themselves over a sense of entitlement and the perfect resume any day.

As Kari Reston, founder and CEO of boredomtoboardroom.com, writes, "Look around — a lot of people in their current roles wouldn't fulfill every criterion that's listed in the job description, so take it with a pinch of salt, and definitely go for it even if you're not a cookie cutter fit for the description.[8]"

I also find it troubling that women will avoid applying for a position if their friend is also interested in it. One time, a co-worker told me with great remorse that she had applied for a job, not realizing her friend coveted the same position.

I get it: no one wants to be branded a job thief, if there even is such a thing. And being considerate of others is a wonderful quality. But I told her — just as I'm telling you — don't take that thoughtfulness so far that you shortchange yourself. There's nothing wrong with pursuing opportunities you think you're suited for. Being honest with your friend about your intentions is really all you owe her.

I'm not advocating lying or padding your resume, but no employer really expects you to tick off every qualification they're looking for. If you think you'd enjoy and excel in a position, apply for it and let the hiring manager make the decision. Companies have been known to adjust their criteria for a candidate who seems perfect to the hiring manager otherwise. A word of caution, though: if the ad asks for five years of experience, and you just graduated, that may be too big a gap to overcome. Still, sending a resume with a knock-out cover letter that shows your potential and desire to learn may be a good way to get noticed — and remembered – when something more suitable comes up.

A few years ago, I applied for the same position as a friend, who just happened to be the company's Golden Boy — a favored employee whose star was clearly on the rise. I called him ahead of time and told him what I was doing. We had a nice chuckle, figuring this was bound to happen at some point, and agreed that both of us would be great at the job. Relationship saved. And you know what? Neither one of us were hired.

If you're struggling with this whole concept, just remember — you're not the decider. You're only asking to be considered. What's more, it is unlikely that for any position there will only be two applicants — you and your pal. Even if you don't apply for the job, he or she might not get it, either. And if you both apply for it and neither of you gets the call, you'll have someone to join you in sorrow-drowning chocolate cake and lattes (or iced teas).

Conversation Starters

Have you been in a situation where your attitude or enthusiasm meant more than your experience?

Share your reaction to the following statement: you can teach a skill; you can't teach nice.

Wendy's Way to Success: Don't Put Yourself in a Box

When I was 10, my fifth-grade teacher said to me that she thought I'd make a great teacher someday. I know she meant it as a compliment, and I did like and respect my teachers, but instead of feeling flattered I was confused. What bothered me, even as a grade-schooler, was the idea that someone was putting me in a box. Her remark made me want to be anything BUT a teacher, in fact.

Our entire lives, we're confronted with "shoulds" and "should nots." You're pretty, you should be a model. You're smart, you should be in Silicon Valley. You're a woman, you shouldn't expect to become a leader in a male-dominated industry.

But who is telling you those things? Who is setting the expectation? And is it the appropriate expectation for you? Only you can decide that, right? Throughout my career, I've found it useful to let go of expectations others have of me — and explore and experiment, instead.

I also like this approach: having a variety of options for the future.

It is still important to have a particular goal or destination in mind, but believing there is only one path to that point can lead to disappointment. Why not consider a couple of strategies for achieving your goals? Leaning on friends or colleagues you can trust to talk through what those strategies might look like can also help.

Let me offer a personal example: one time a woman asked me if I thought she should apply for a more senior position. She was a well-accomplished person, but despite her abilities and experience, she said she felt totally unprepared for the role she really wanted. Rather than focusing on her achievements, she rattled off a list of the jobs she hadn't held that she thought were essential for the senior-level position she aspired to. I had one simple question for her: who told you those were the jobs required to get where you want to go?

It had never occurred to her that this prescribed course for success didn't really even exist. She had the option of applying for her dream position, letting the decision maker (the hiring manager) do her job, and seeing what happened next.

I've mentioned before, I wouldn't be where I am if not for some disappointments and setbacks, some exploration, and experiments. I have been turned down for more jobs than I've been offered. And when I moved between companies, I accepted a downgrade in my role, believing that my abilities and the quality of my work would be apparent soon enough, and then I would be rewarded. And that is exactly what happened: I was made a vice president within seven years. I think it's also important to note that during those seven years, I took two lateral career moves, retaining the same level and job title, without any assurance of what would come next. One of those moves even meant transplanting my family outside of the United States. I know there are plenty of people who wouldn't make a geographic change like that unless it was accompanied by a promotion or a guarantee of some sort.

But let's face it: the next level is never guaranteed. It would be great if our career journey was always a smooth, clear path. But we learn a lot from rocky parts and roadblocks, like perseverance, patience, and how much inner strength we really have — things that are every bit as useful outside the office as in.

Pack Your Bags and Move On

Whether you are looking for your first job, ready to move up, or considering changing companies or careers, it's comforting to think that there is a defined path ahead of you. We're taught to believe that if we do X, Y, and Z — in that order and to the best of our ability — we will get to where we want to go.

But even with the best intentions and most deliberate preparation, sometimes, there are just things we cannot control. In my case, the X factor was my age. Or, rather, my youth.

It was the mid-2000s, and I was a financial reporting manager for a major airline, responsible for preparing all of the Security Exchange Commission-required reports. I loved the industry and the flight benefits that came along with it. I was willing to do just about anything for the company, including working for a salary well below market rates and even hanging in through a pay cut.

The airline was part owner of a Central America-based regional carrier that had decided to do an initial public offering (IPO). When I learned that the carrier needed help with SEC filings, including the reports related to an acquisition of a smaller company, I jumped at the chance to be involved. In true "put me in, Coach" style (by that, I mean Coach, the team leader, not coach, the part of the plane), I begged our controller to let me make the trip to Panama. I could have my bags packed tonight and be en route tomorrow, I said. Finally, he gave me the go-ahead.

It's fair to say that I was thrilled. I would get to experience another country, meet new people, and try to help another company.

But once on the ground in Panama, I realized I had overlooked something that might affect my eventual success: I didn't speak Spanish. Oops, right? Fortunately, a bilingual colleague was dispatched a few hours later. The rest, I figured, would be smooth sailing. I mean, what could be more difficult than a language barrier?

Unfortunately, that wasn't the only problem I encountered. And the next one was a whole heck of a lot tougher to fix.

Performing an accounting coup made me a rock star in my company. But it still didn't guarantee a promotion. What held me back was something I had no control over: my age. There are ways to overcome a lack of education or poor interview skills, but you can't change your birthdate. There will be times when you realize you've reached a dead end, even in a job you love, and it will be time to move on. Maybe you need more money. Maybe the work is interfering with your family life. Maybe you're too young for a promotion. It won't be easy — changes never are, even when they're for the best — but do the best you can to leave on good terms. Finish up your assignments, give enough notice, and provide ways for your co-workers to keep in touch.

The tax and cash flow documents provided by the smaller company were a straight-up disaster, to put it mildly. Despite their best efforts, the regional carrier's accounting team couldn't make sense of them. To be honest, I was equally perplexed. When I called our controller to tell him about the mess, his response was to try to bring me home: "You gave it a good shot. We can say you did everything you could."

Not so fast, I thought. I was determined that taxes were not going to get the best of me. I worked around the clock to fix the problem, refusing to believe that we couldn't figure this thing out. Accounting isn't rocket science, after all. And when everyone else thinks something can't be done, I'm the one who says, "Yes, it can."

So, we took a deep breath and wiped the taxes clean and started over, recreating all of the accounts.

With the revised reports filed, the IPO went through.

Yes, I was a bit of a rock star at the airline. I received the highest performance rating they gave and a swanky trip that included travel on their inaugural flight to Buenos Aires.

I was certain that when I returned I'd be promoted. I envisioned an even-more responsible job with a salary to match.

Instead, I heard this: "We looked for a new, higher-level position for you, but you're too young."

Despite what was clearly meant to be a rejection, my first reaction was actually happiness: at least my accomplishments had been recognized, and I was being considered for a promotion. Maybe, I told myself, they were still looking for a better spot for me, regardless of my youth.

But then, as one week turned into two, and two into three, and work life went back to normal, it hit me like a ton of bricks. I couldn't change my age. And the company wasn't going to change the way they felt about my youth. I recognized with much pain and some tears that it was time to leave the airline.

If you are not progressing the way you hoped or planned for, it's important to understand what is actually holding you back. Is it something you can influence or change? For example, do you need more education? Are your interview skills shaky? Do you find it difficult to stay late at the office to work on extra projects that might get you noticed? Are you afraid to ask for more responsibility or embarrassed to ask for help?

There are solutions for each of those obstacles. They may not be easy, and it may take some soul-searching, but with motivation, willpower, and guidance, it is possible to overcome them.

Sometimes, though, what is keeping us from moving forward is something we have no control over at all. And then, our best option may be to cut our losses, pack our bags, and move on.

To this day, I count solving this accounting issue as one of my greatest work accomplishments. It's regrettable that it was followed by my career at the airline ending. I had overcome obstacles that other accountants wouldn't have been willing to tackle, but that didn't guarantee my path.

Now that I have the benefit of time and perspective, though, I can see the positives that came from my decision to accept reality and move on. In fact, my next stop was a position with the company I work for today. I'm not saying that every detour will lead to something better. But refusing to recognize unwinnable situations can be a dead end.

Conversation Starters

**Have you ever judged someone by their age?
How did that affect your experience with them?**

In general, how would you (honestly) rate your acceptance of change? Are you excited, does it scare you, or are you somewhere in the middle?

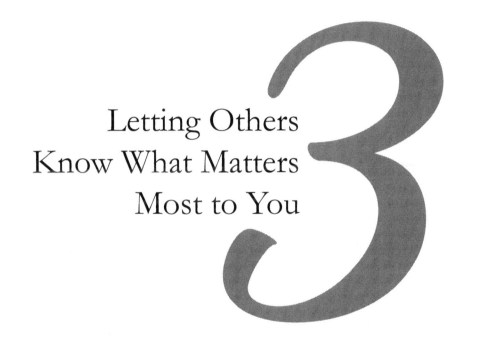

Letting Others
Know What Matters
Most to You

We Talk, We Lead

CHAPTER 3: LETTING OTHERS KNOW WHAT MATTERS MOST TO YOU

Yes, it can feel like a tightwire act sometimes, but I'm here to tell you: workplace success does not have to come at the expense of what matters most in your life. You don't have to lose yourself, neglect important people, or give up the activities you love in order to achieve your work goals.

*You can probably find hundreds of suggestions out there about how to realize work-life balance, from meditating to **not** multi-tasking. Some writers suggest cutting back to a 40-hour week (!), leaving your briefcase at the office a few times a week, or simply refusing to work weekends.*

What has worked best for me is prioritizing what matters most, expressing loud and clear what my priorities are, and learning how to say no when someone tries to infringe on what is important to me.

Of course, I feel it's only right to give the same space and consideration to my team members. I respect that their families come first and that time with spouses, partners, and family is sacred. In fact, I actually see it as my responsibility to help protect the time they spend together. The payoff is happy employees with no hidden resentments and a pleasant, productive workplace.

On Balance, a Better Way to Work

Regardless of where we are in our careers, working women have this in common: we're constantly walking a tightwire trying to balance the requirements of our jobs with the other demands in our lives. I think we can agree it's a challenge to keep our work hours from overlapping with what should be our free time, especially in a hyper-connected world where bosses who have no boundaries, but access to a computer or cell phone, can contact us at any time.

One solution: learning to say NO.

I know that finding the fortitude to say no is a roadblock for many women. Listen to what writer Suzanne Gerber says about it: "Even for the most stalwart women, there comes a moment when our inner resolve fails us, and one of the simplest sounds in the English language (n-o) comes out as 'OK,' 'sure,' 'why not,' 'all right,' 'I suppose,' 'if you really think so' — or just as a sigh of resignation.'"

Do you recognize yourself? I know that I used to fit that profile pretty darned well.

Fortunately, the days when I felt compelled to constantly say yes are now largely behind me, and that's thanks to my husband. He helped me realize that it's impossible for me to make everyone happy all of the time, no matter how much I want to or how hard I try. My priorities, as only I can define them, are what have to come first. That's why they're called priorities, right?

Actually, my husband and son get a lot of credit for making me the leader I am today and contributing to the success of my career. From small, simple acts to sweeping gestures, they've exhibited their faith and trust in me in so many ways, not least of which is my husband, Matt's, confidence that uprooting our family and moving to Canada for my job would be a good move.

Here are a few examples of what I mean.

Just two months after we married, I was assigned to a project where, for a year-and-a-half, I would split my time 50-50 between Houston and Canada. Here we were, newlyweds, and I was going to be gone half of the next 18 months. My husband could have resisted, argued against, or even tried to block the change. Instead, he encouraged me, making a point of taking me to the airport each time I had to leave for Canada and picking me up when I returned, usually with an iced tea in hand, which is more welcoming to me than roses.

My husband has been endlessly supportive of me. He and my son are my priorities. My team members know that, just as I know their families come first for them, too. An environment where boundaries are respected is essential to work-life balance. As a leader, I model positive behaviors for my team to help them achieve the right balance: that includes NOT being available around the clock. I don't want to answer an email at 2 a.m., and I don't expect anyone else to do it, either. Vacation time is sacred for me and my team members — they don't even have to ask for time off, although they must let me know what kind of help will be required in their absence to keep their work on track. I'm honest about my needs, and I encourage that same level of honesty from my team. If we've let each other know who we are all along, we've probably already developed a short-cut for understanding one another.

Now, you may be thinking, "that's the very least a spouse could do." But he had no requirement to play chauffeur. He told me that this was his way of maximizing the time we spent together, which is a pretty sweet sentiment. And even more than that, it showed me he supported this phase of my career, which helped to temper the sadness I felt about leaving him for weeks at a time.

But that's not all. During those months when Canada was socked in with snow and the daily forecast promised only more insanely cold weather, he took over much of the traveling, coming to see me so I could avoid germy planes and stay healthy for work. Pretty great, right?

As you might imagine, his big-hearted support continued after the assignment was completed and our marriage matured. I'll never forget — and always appreciate — when, a few years later, he drove an eight-month-pregnant me to night MBA classes so I could accomplish my goal of completing my courses that semester.

With all he does for me, it might be easy to take my husband's help and encouragement for granted. I work hard to make sure that doesn't happen. In fact, I make it my priority to be there for him and my son in the same, selfless way. Because being a wife and mother are a big part of who I am, being genuinely Wendy includes letting everyone know that my husband and son take precedence over everything else. In fact, that was a key point in the getting-to-know-me presentation for my team members when I became the leader of the finance department: "Team members take priority over myself and my work, but not my family."

That's not to say I haven't had to make some sacrifices for my job. I've made choices that have kept me from eating breakfast with my son or reading him a bedtime story. But the big things, like his piano recitals or soccer games or birthdays, are non-negotiable. And date nights with my husband? We sometimes have to sync them on our smart phones, but we have them. I book a babysitter — typically one from my vetted pool of colleagues' kids; it makes us feel good to know that we are paying a responsible kid some extra spending money — even if we don't have anything planned.

But those decisions are mine, not someone else's. Because I've made my limits obvious, people know what to expect from me. That's why I didn't feel I had to hide the reason I skipped a big company dinner a while back. I'd been spending a lot of time at the office and, plain and simple, I wanted to see my son.

I realize it's not easy to make our needs known, especially because as women we tend to be obedient, responsible rule-followers — in other words, people-pleasers. However, as Nigel Marsh, author of *Fat, Forty, and Fired*, explains, if we don't take responsibility for the type of life we want to lead, someone else — like our boss — may do it for us... and we may not like their idea of balance.[10]

OK, all you people-pleasers, let me blow your mind: ***standing up for ourselves is not only good for us, it actually helps our company.***

How? Well, a workaholic environment that keeps us away from people we love and forces us to give up things we enjoy, like hobbies, sports, or therapeutic naps, leads to resentment and anger. That prevents us from performing at our best. Study after study shows that being overworked is bad for us. It harms efficiency, hinders creativity and good judgment, and increases the likelihood of mistakes.

Those are some of the reasons why I feel my job as a leader is not just to protect time for what matters most to *me*, but also to create an environment where my team members have the same privilege. I respect that their hours away from the office are their own and should not be interrupted or infringed upon. Take, for example, one of my highly valued, high-achieving direct reports. He'll go on vacation but continue to send work emails like crazy. Of course, I appreciate his dedication. But enough is enough, and it's my job to tell him so. After the second or third email, I will text him: "STOP. I'm here, and I can cover your work. Enjoy your time off, and don't let me see another email from you until you're back in the office."

The upshot is that my team members enjoy better balance in their lives. They aren't harboring some hidden (or more obvious) bitterness about being at work, and their happiness translates into a pleasant and productive workplace. By the same token, because I set my own boundaries between family time and work, my team members know that when we're together, they're getting my undivided attention — 100 percent Wendy, 100 percent of the time.

Conversation Starters

How do you let the people around you know what matters most to you?

Have you ever been pleasantly surprised by the outcome of saying no?

What little extras do your family members do to show their support of your career?

When Time Means More Than Money

As professional women with demanding schedules, we realize that time is currency — and it's often more valuable than money. After all, whether we're making a living or a peanut butter sandwich for our kids, things take time. And there's only so much (or so little) of it. As we try to balance work and life, there are occasions when we have to tip the scales toward spending some money because it saves us time.

For example, as a wife and mother, I love being in charge of the celebrations in my husband's and son's lives. But no one said I have to do everything myself.

Yes, I know that with only a few (hundred) clicks on Pinterest, I could pull off a child's birthday that would rival a royal wedding. But thinking of the hours I'd spend baking from scratch and folding origami paper into woodland creatures makes my head hurt and my fingers cramp up. I'm not suggesting that my family doesn't deserve the fun that a well-organized party represents. It's just that the fun can happen even if someone else does the heavy lifting.

That's why I have a local restaurant on speed-dial. They're the experts in cooking, baking, serving, and cleaning up afterward, and I feel no shame outsourcing those sorts of things.

Do I hear horrified gasps? I get it — high-achievers might find it tough to admit they can't do it all. I think that's why, like me, many female leaders are reluctant to divulge the fact they hire someone to keep their homes tidy — it's sort of admitting to a weakness, like we can't manage our time or we're careless. But I say, come clean (in the figurative sense): no one is good at everything, is expected to be, or has the time for it, especially if we spend long hours on the clock and want to relax and enjoy our families in our off time. At the office, I don't feel bad that I can't write a media release as well as our communications people do. And I bet they aren't upset that they can't produce an accurate balance sheet. We all have our strengths: I might not be able to craft a homemade gift, but if you need someone to find the perfect place to host your next brunch, I'm your girl. My attitude is that there's no point adding stress to your life — and missing out on precious family time — trying to do things that other people excel at and do for a living. Why not enlist their help instead?

Case in point: my son's holiday cookie-decorating party.

A few weeks before Christmas, he made a modest request: to invite some friends over to frost cookies. What a sweet, old-fashioned idea.

His proposal meant a lot to me. As in *a lot* of buying supplies, baking, straightening up, and trimming the house. All activities that would further cut into the time I have to spend with him.

Instead of adding to my already full plate, I booked a few hours for the party at a local hotel. You might think that's a pretty institutional environment for a kids' event, but the place was decked for the holidays and couldn't have been more festive. And, to be honest, unless you're Eloise at the Plaza, getting to spend an afternoon in a hotel ballroom is actually quite a grown-up kind of treat when you're 5, 6, or 7.

Let's face it: no one is good at everything. There's no point in adding stress trying to do what others excel at when you can get their help instead. Don't let anyone tell you that you have to do it all yourself or it doesn't count; there's no shame in outsourcing. Think of it this way: do you fill all the roles in your department or company? Unless you're a one-woman show, probably not — and even then, you might still get support from an IT person or tax accountant. So what makes you think you have to do EVERYTHING at home? If you stay up all night baking that cake or sewing that recital costume, what will you be the next day, other than exhausted? Is that good for your productivity or mood? Of course not. To me, it's more important to be fully present for the people who need us than to be frazzled trying to do the behind-the-scenes work and then just phoning in an appearance.

The catering department made the cookies and set up a decorating station, and some friends who are ardent DIYers helped the young guests make Christmas crafts. We ate, listened to holiday music, took photos, played Duck-Duck-Goose, and everyone left happy and, maybe, slightly sticky.

Oh, sure, I heard a little background noise about hosting the party at a hotel. But you know what? No matter what I do, some people support me and some people don't. In this case, I was willing to spend a little more money than I probably would have on a home party because it saved me time (and likely turned out better than if I had staged it all myself). But most important, it allowed me to keep my commitment to my son that he could have a memorable and fun cookie-decorating party. Because I wasn't stressed out or running around like a crazy woman, I could be fully present at his party. And that was a gift to both of us.

Conversation Starters

Have you ever shelled out big bucks to prevent adding more work to your to-do list? Did you feel guilty or relieved?

Do you often find yourself needing to justify your actions to co-workers or even friends, especially regarding home/housework? Why do you think that's the case?

Is Pinterest a source of inspiration... or stress?

Welcome to the Club (the Women with Families Club, That Is)

According to data from The World Bank, in 2017, 56 percent of the American workforce were women (for Canada, the percentage was higher at 61 percent).[11]

Those figures, and the fact that workplaces are increasingly multicultural, *should* mean that the days of the old boys' club — when white men dominated the world of work and decided who would be successful — are over.

But that males-only mentality creeps in more often than we probably would like to admit.

And sometimes, it shows up in the oddest places.

For example, I have noticed it at company charity auctions when items like hockey tickets or a round of golf with a male executive are put on the block.

Although these "experiences" typically attract some high bidders, I think they also prevent a lot of people from participating. And that's not just because the winning price is exorbitant or some people dislike sports. To my mind, they can leave women feeling left out. And that can happen in two ways.

First, there are plenty of women who will never feel comfortable spending time on the links or at the rink — or anywhere else, for that matter — with a man who wields power over them at work, regardless of how well they know him. (Of course, the reverse is probably also true: men might balk at the idea of being alone in a social setting with a woman they work for.)

And second, for anyone with a family, an outing with an executive takes away hours that could be devoted to their spouse and children, instead.

I can't keep men from offering the auction items they do, and I wouldn't even try. Those things are traditions in many companies, and I know that they raise an awful lot of money in mine. What I can do, however, is be more sensitive to the audience. For me, that means recognizing and respecting the fact that if I'm auctioning an experience or event, it will cut into an individual's private time. As a result, I tailor my donations so they include not just the employee, but his or her family, too.

Businesses give a lot of lip service to the "employees come first; they're our most important asset" message. But I think it's better to demonstrate it. Companies already ask employees to spend enough time away from their families, so I work to create opportunities for families to be together — and for couples to have some alone time. By showing my team members that I understand their priorities — which, in large part, are my own — they feel valued and accepted. They are happier and more productive. And because I'm not making demands that dominate the team members' free time, their families are likely to be more understanding when occasions arise that do keep them apart.

So far, I've had a lot of success offering family dinners at my house and days at the beach with me, my husband, and my son. I did make an exception one time, auctioning a breakfast with me for the employee only. Although it was an early morning event, it was scheduled to protect getting-the-kids-ready-for-school time.

I've also discovered that sometimes, it seems like the fact that employees have families hasn't even been considered. For example, every year my company sponsors a big cultural grand opening event 110 miles away from our offices, and just about everyone who attends stays overnight. I was apparently the first person *ever* to ask if there would be childcare available there. Locating babysitters at the venue hadn't even crossed the minds of the event planners, who told me they had assumed everyone could easily make arrangements or had family who could watch their kids. Not me. I was new to the community and didn't have a relative within a thousand miles. But you know what? When they offered onsite childcare, I was hardly the only one to sign up.

Which brings us to another topic, which is the well-deserved break from the children that yes, we *all* need and appreciate. I recognize that a night away from the kids is a special — and possibly rare — treat for a lot of people. I have had opportunities to help some of my team members actually carve out time with their spouses — like when I invited my direct reports and their husbands and wives to dinner followed by a charity event. In a work world that seemingly does everything it can to keep people chained to their desks, this was one way I could help these couples let loose — get dressed up, act like grown-ups, and enjoy some time together. The charity benefited, of course, but I heard the pay-off for the couples in their comments: that they were grateful for the rare night out and appreciated being with other adults.

Is caring this much about something like an auction item or similar issue overblown? I don't think so. Instead, it's a small, subtle gesture that makes a huge impact — to show what's important to me, and, more to the point, that I share the priorities of people at my stage in life. If this is our club, we want as many folks as possible to feel welcome.

Conversation Starters

How does having a family change the value you bring to your company?

Does your company make "family" feel important?

Doing Business
Like a Woman

We Talk, We Lead

CHAPTER 4: DOING BUSINESS LIKE A WOMAN

Olga Khazan, writing in The Atlantic, *describes a Pew Research study that asked 2,002 people if they preferred working with men or women. Of those who had a preference, twice as many said they would rather work for a man. And more women than men said they'd rather work for a man: "Among women, some studies make it seem as though this preference is the professional extension of 'all my best friends are guys.*[12]*'"*

In other words, women don't think female personalities are that appealing and they would prefer to surround themselves with men.

Ouch.

Men, it seems, are more straight-talking and less prone to moods. As Simone Milasas, Joy of Business founder, says, "A man's way is often direct. He want to get straight to the point and give or receive information and then make a choice.[13]*"*

Women, on the other hand, are likely to talk about things at greater length, discuss how things could work, and ask, "what do you think about this?"

That description fits me pretty well. I am a communicator who favors collaboration. If those are feminine qualities, then fine — I'm a woman so it's no surprise that I have them. I'll even confess that my penchant for teamwork and cooperation has been mistaken for weakness or a lack of confidence or decision-making ability.

I've succeeded by using my strengths as a woman, including my apparently gender-specific preference for being collaborative. But it hasn't always been easy to navigate the male-dominated work world I'm in or know exactly what the rules are. As author Gail Evans said, "Men know the rules because they wrote them.[14]"

The Only Kind of Leader I Can Be

"You're the first woman I didn't mind working for."

I suppose that's not the most ringing endorsement ever — the man who said it to me might have substituted "enjoyed" for something a bit more positive rather than the ho-hum phrase, "I didn't mind."

But I imagine the subtext to his comment was this: he'd had female bosses before who, in his estimation, were unpleasant to work for. Somehow, I was an exception.

I can't know for sure what made him think I was different or better, but it could be that I strive to put everyone around me at ease, and he sensed that. I realize that women have a reputation for being tough to work for, and I try with every fiber of my being not to justify that notion.

Still, the only kind of leader I can be is a female leader. I can't put on a masculine mask and spend every working day pretending to be something I'm not. I have to be comfortable in my own skin.

So, what is a female leader like me to do?

Well, for one thing, I feel it's my place to prove that women can work well together. In a male-dominated corporate environment where women have to compete over a few available leadership spots, female rivalry is often alive and kicking (if you'll pardon the image).

I feel I have a responsibility to prove that women can work well together and support each other. As a role model for other women, I can prove that it is better when we function as a team rather than as adversaries or rivals. Women might be afraid of sticking together when they want to stand out, but only we understand what it is like to try to succeed and advance in a male-dominated corporate environment. And it is essential that we share the stories of how we have progressed so we can inspire each other. I have heard about women who hid their marriages, obscured their pregnancies, or wouldn't display their children's artwork, all for the sake of fitting into a male business culture. I say we need to use our female qualities to change culture and make the workplace more open and accepting for everyone.

For me, though, the work world would be a cold and lonely place if there weren't other women to share it with.

Yet, I've heard all sorts of crazy things about whether my company's other female executive and I can cooperate with one another, from, "Are you upset there's another woman at the table?" (uh, no, of course not) to "I'm glad you're getting along" (yes, isn't it good to see us playing nicely? Sigh). The fact is, we truly are each other's biggest cheerleaders. When she was promoted to vice president, I was probably the happiest person in the company — well, right behind her, of course. We've sent each other flowers to mark both joyous and difficult occasions, and the Wonder Woman sticker on my bulletin board came from her. We are each other's sounding board and behind-the-scenes supporter.

I also think it's important for me to be a role model for other women. I can show them that it's OK to be fun and funny and soft-hearted and to admit their failings — and that cooperation and collaboration aren't signs of weakness but expressions of trust. I can prove that we benefit most when we combine everyone's gifts. As *Profit First* author Michael Michalowicz points out, "Your company will function better as a team than as adversaries.[15]"

And, finally, I can use that feminine quality of empathy to better understand the business styles of those around me. Simone Milasas encourages women to see beyond social pressures and expectations, and to embrace our natural business style. I think we improve the workplace when we return the favor and respond to others in a way that acknowledges their style as well.

I like to think I've created a culture where people can flourish and have significant opportunities to achieve. The proof of my success is that my team is composed entirely of high-performing, high-potential individuals — and they are helping me become the type of leader no one minds working for.

Conversation Starters

Women have a reputation for being tough to work for. In your experience, is that justified?

Regardless of whether being a woman has helped or hindered you in your career, what kind of compromises have you had to make?

How have you shown support for the other women around you?

It's on Me. Or, Is It on You?

One night last winter, I went to dinner with two female audit partners from my company's consulting firm. Although we'd set out just to enjoy one another's company, predictably the conversation turned to work. After all, work is what we had in common.

Still, the evening remained generally light-hearted. When the check came, we even joked that one of the audit partners should pick up the tab, instead of us dividing it. I was the client, after all. Maybe they should be treating me.

And then it dawned on us: it may have been funny, but there was truth underlying the humor.

What we realized, almost simultaneously, is that if we were three men under the same circumstances, one of us — most likely one of the audit partners — would have expensed the entire bill. Regardless of the amount of business talk that transpired, there would have been no doubt that this had been a working dinner.

So, why did three smart, strong women have to stop and think about it? Why was it that the implicit etiquette that says when business associates go out together, one of the companies will pay — an unwritten rule that seems secondhand to men — feel like it didn't apply to us?

On the ride home, we dug a little deeper into the check-paying puzzle.

Here's what we decided.

The biggest issue was that even though we knew work topics would come up, we hadn't framed the meal as a business dinner. There was no agenda, no desired outcome, and no set purpose. It was not for team building or development, or to debrief after a big meeting or trip to a business unit.

A man might not care about any of those distinctions, figuring anytime the guys from work are together — even on the golf course or eating wings and watching football — it's a business thing. Which isn't to suggest that men are less ethical or more inclined to try to pull one over on the system. It has more to do with the way men make decisions, which, according to science, is influenced by tradition.[16] And if tradition says that when a group of guys from the office get together, one expenses the meal, well then, so be it.

Why didn't one of us expense the dinner check? The evening didn't fit our definition of a business meeting, so we weren't willing to charge it to any of our companies. But you know what? A man would have. Men make decisions based on tradition, rules, and regulations, while women are more likely to be inquisitive and cooperative. Sometimes, cooperation and collaboration are considered signs of weakness, a willingness to agree even when your best interests and instincts would scream, "No, no, no!" But researchers have found that collaborative thinkers are well-suited for positions where it is important to consider multiple stakeholders. That means the typical female decision-making style is right for the C-level suite and the boardroom.

Following old-fashioned norms about picking up the check is one thing. But when tradition is the basis for corporate decision making, the outcome is often less than stellar. That's where thinking like, "we've always done it that way" can interfere with progress and innovation.

The good news is women are less likely to rely on traditional ways of decision making. In the workplace, at least, we aren't always bound to rules, particularly when those rules make cooperation or collaboration — two things we value — more difficult. We're likely to be more inquisitive than men at work, and to consider the interests of all stakeholders before settling on a conclusion.

What this suggests is that women's decision-making skills are well suited for managerial positions, C-level suites, and the boardroom — as well as for making working life more enjoyable for those around them, if you ask me.

Now, this might seem like a lot of deep thinking stemming from a shared dinner tab. But clearly, the experience illustrates some of the key differences between men and women in the workplace (and the world) and why no one grabbed the check. In essence, the evening didn't fit our more defined view of a business meeting. We thought it was just a chance for women who'd met at work to get together on our own time and catch up with one another.

But you know what? Regardless of who the dinner was on, I'm convinced that the time we spent together will reap more benefits in the long term than any organized event ever could. We had made a deliberate choice to be together in our off hours, at a real dinner, re-connecting and building our relationships.

And that has more business value than any expense report could reflect.

Conversation Starters

Why wasn't it natural for us to expense the meal?
Is it the same reason we identified?

A group of male managers leave early to play a round of golf.
At the same time, several female managers head off to a spa.
Would people perceive those actions differently? Why?

You Can't Force Inspiration

I know I've mentioned occasions when I've outsourced my party planning, but the fact is, I really do love surprising people and creating unique ways to build camaraderie and connections, from "sweatworking sessions" to our team's "Name That Song" competitions.

As an example, during my first year in the executive leadership group, we started discussing how we might celebrate the winter holidays together. With objectives like strengthening our bonds, becoming closer as a team, and acknowledging our successes, we started brainstorming.

Remember: I'm talking about a leadership group — our president and all the vice presidents — that is overwhelmingly male. Out of 12 people, only two of us are women.

Although these guys can plan and execute a major business project with seeming ease, throwing a holiday celebration isn't exactly their strong suit. Maybe they find it silly or frivolous or potentially embarrassing. I'll wager they find it a little awkward to buy gifts for one another.

I'm sure you know where this is going. Even though I'm every bit as busy as "the boys," I appointed myself the holiday event planner and said I'd come up with an appropriate gift for the president.

And then I sat back and waited for inspiration to strike.

Now, hearing me say "waiting for inspiration to strike" might seem a little odd to you. For goal-oriented, take-charge women, it's not easy to turn off the impulse to act. If you'd rather do anything than sit and wait for inspiration to come to you, you're hardly alone: a quick Google search shows hundreds of strategies for seeking inspiration, from practicing yoga to watching a TED Talk or drinking caffeine (as if I need another reason to head down the hall for more iced tea).

But for me, inspiration isn't something I can force or find. Instead, I have to let it find me. This approach is something that has evolved over my leadership journey. I find that some of my best ideas come about when I least expect it, like when I am blow drying my hair. Sometimes, after I get a good night's sleep, I wake up with the solution to a problem I was working on for hours the day before. It took a while, but I have finally learned to trust myself enough to know that inspiration will find me and I do not have to force it. It is not something that was easy to do at first, but now it is habit.

In the case of figuring out what to do for our leadership group's holiday celebration, it happened on an airport tarmac.

It was a beautiful day, and we were all walking out to the plane heading back to head office after a long, two-day strategy session, rolling bags behind us.

Don't we all feel like superheroes, someone laughingly asked.

AHA! There was my inspiration. When we returned, I commissioned a graphic designer to create a poster featuring superhero likenesses of each of us, which was framed and presented to the president at our — you guessed it — superhero-themed party. The dozen of us played a gift exchange game that included a Christmas poem I'd written, personalized to our business. You should have seen the guys tearing into their presents — ornaments, t-shirts, socks, everything embellished or emblazoned with a superhero — with the kind of zeal usually reserved for an NHL hockey match.

If you're thinking, "Wendy, how did you get roped into this party-planning role; isn't that the very definition of women's work, which we're trying to avoid as we progress in our careers?" the fact is, I took it upon myself because I wanted to. I thought it would be a great opportunity to have some fun together, get a break from the pressure swirling around us and grow closer as a team. If putting together an event falls under the category of women's work, it might be just because we're the creative and capable ones, right? I wasn't worried that organizing the party would in any way diminish me or my role in the eyes of my colleagues. (For that matter, I'll be the one who grabs food for everyone to eat on the corporate jet. Not because I'm a woman but because I'm hungry and figure the guys are, too. I suppose being thoughtful is a more feminine quality, but that doesn't mean it's bad!)

After the holiday party, I heard nothing but positive comments, from "I can't recall the last time we did presents" to "thank you for letting me remember what it's like to feel surprised."

When I let go and step back from micromanaging situations, creative inspiration seems to be everywhere! That is how our executives became superheroes for our holiday party. Yes, it's tough to avoid nagging a problem to death, but sometimes, after a good night's sleep, I'll wake up with the answer that eluded me the day before. You have to trust yourself to know that inspiration will find you and you don't have to force it.

Here was the kind of activity a group made up mostly of men loved participating in, yet it's not something they would have ever organized for themselves. It took a women being willing to come forward, become inspired, organize all of the moving parts, and not be afraid to do something different, to make it happen.

So what happened when the holidays rolled around again? Was it assumed that I would take on the party planning again?

In fact, I did set things in motion by asking the leadership group for their ideas about activities and the gift we should get for our president. But then an amazing thing occurred: other people began stepping up — and I quickly learned they'd stepped up their game from the previous year. One suggested a perfect keepsake present. Another offered to be in charge of "fun." A third planned a group boxing class for the morning of the party. And me? I didn't have to lift a finger.

Recognizing there was value to the previous holiday party had inspired them. Yes, it had taken an example of how well things could turn out before everyone bought into the idea. But we all know you can't just expect change by ripping off the bandage: that can sting even superheroes.

Conversation Starters

Where do you do your best brainstorming?

Can you recall a time when you felt compelled to take on "women's work" because you were the only female colleague (or you didn't trust the guys to handle it)?

Win, Lose,
or Draw

We Talk, We Lead

CHAPTER 5: WIN, LOSE, OR DRAW

"Aim higher and negotiate better.[17]*" By doing two things, says the U.S. Department of Labor, women will be able to close the gender-wage gap.*

If only life were that simple.

Women and the way we negotiate has been a subject of considerable study and discussion as more of us entered the workforce and, especially, began achieving higher-level positions. Where "coming on strong" used to be the chief negotiating tactic for many high-powered women, that approach has been tempered in recent years. Jennifer Pereira, at the time a principal in direct private equity at the CPP Investment Board, was quoted in a 2015 article about women and negotiating. She said that her early attitude was, "I have to win, I have to be right, I have to show that I'm right." She soon learned, she said, that there's "more than one way to be right... At the end of the day it's about being open and collaborating.[18]*"*

I am a self-professed not-very-good negotiator. But I'm trying to up my game. I've started practicing with some low-risk negotiations. For one, I asked our corporate real estate department to redecorate a conference space. In the back of my mind, I was willing to foot the entire bill. But when I wound up splitting the costs, instead it seemed like a win for me —and everyone else, too.

And next time, I will aim higher and negotiate better.

Negotiating on My Own Terms

When it comes to negotiation, women have met the enemy, and it is us.

At least that's the view according to women who have studied the subject, like writer Linda Babcock.

As a woman who would rank my own negotiation skills as poor, I take some comfort in the fact that I'm not alone. But I wonder: why are we so bad at it?

Babcock found that women make a lot of mistakes when it comes to negotiating.

First, she says, we don't know how to persuasively ask for what we want.

Second, we have lower expectations than men do. That means we get less not because we're women, but because we ask for less.

Finally, we worry that negotiating will be harmful to our reputations — and, I might add, our relationships. (The research, by the way, shows this concern is real. When women tried to negotiate for higher salaries or more benefits, they were penalized by both male and female hiring managers. You're right: it's not fair. But there is a work-around, which I'll get to in a bit.)[19]

Recently, my ability to negotiate was tested by a white, windowless room.

Well, by paying to have it decorated, actually.

Here's what happened.

Our corporate offices are in a building where function is clearly more important than beauty. In the basement — which we refer to as the ground floor in order to make going down there less bleak — are conference rooms. White-walled, windowless conference rooms, or as I like to call it, "corporate jail," but with video technology.

The space is supposed to be where cooperation and creativity take place. But I can't find inspiration in a room like that. I figured that others, inside the finance department and out, felt the same way.

Clearly, it was time for a makeover.

I talked to the folks in both the public affairs and corporate real estate departments about doing what I politely called a "refresh," including adding new paint, new artwork, and company messaging on the walls.

We're all so proud of the company, I said. Our conference rooms should reflect that.

Heads nodded all around and everyone agreed. I shared my ideas with the executive leadership group, who admitted they didn't even realize it needed to be done until I'd brought it up, but now the white room where we met was driving some of them crazy, too.

The only problem was no one had anticipated doing a conference room refresh when we developed our annual budgets. So, who should pay for this much-needed project? I had suggested it, but my department isn't the only one using the conference rooms.

The real estate group seemed friendly, so I decided to try out my negotiation skills and see how much they would chip in. This was a low-risk "practice" negotiation for me — I really had nothing to lose. If, like me, you're not comfortable negotiating, it's better to start with something lower risk before you go into something tough, like salary talks.

In the back of my mind, I was ready to cover all of the costs. But the real estate team surprised me by saying they'd foot the entire bill. We like you and what you're trying to do, they said.

Now, a man would have replied, "OK, thanks," and walked away.

I, however, couldn't take yes for an answer. I felt bad sticking them with the entire expense, and offered to split the costs 50-50.

Before you think this was another negotiation fail for Wendy — that I could have gotten away without spending a dime, but agreed to pay for half of the renovation — the fact is, I walked in willing to cover the entire cost of redoing the room. Getting away with paying 50 percent was a win for me. I didn't have to pay zero to feel I had succeeded.

I'm not the best negotiator, but I'm always looking for ways to improve. One way I practiced my skills was by developing a plan to turn our video-equipped corporate "jail" into a welcoming place for creativity and collaboration. By showing how the change would benefit everyone, not just me, I was able to get the win. Using a cooperative approach — "we" instead of "me" — can help women improve their negotiating ability. Another expert tip is to get into the right frame of mind before you begin a negotiation. Think about when you were assertive and succeeded in the past, and you are more likely to get what you want this time.

Now, back to that workaround I mentioned.

Remember when I said that negotiating can negatively affect our reputation and relationships? It turns out, women can better succeed at negotiating when they position what they want not in their best interest, but in the interest of someone or something else.

Hannah Riley Bowles, a senior lecturer at Harvard's Kennedy School of Government and the director of the Women in Power program, is quoted in *The New Yorker*: "We've found that you need to offer an explanation for your demands that gives a legitimate reason that the other side finds persuasive." She also adds, "You need to signal concern for the broader organization: 'It's not just good for me; it's good for you.[20]'"

That's exactly the approach I took in the case of the ghostly, ghastly conference room. Initially, I may have been the only one it bothered or the only one willing to speak up about it. But by framing the refresh as something that tied into company pride, others could buy into it. Getting the work done would benefit the entire organization. And it has: now, we have a conference room where meetings don't feel like incarcerations. We're happier and more productive.

And although I was ready to pay for the entire refresh, getting to share in the expense instead taught me that I could negotiate like a woman and reach my goals.

Conversation Starters

What is your most successful, or most memorable, negotiation?

Why might you have a harder time with financial negotiations?

Do You Know What You Are Really Worth?

If you are anything like me, you set pretty high standards for yourself. You put in long hours, don't cut corners; you give it your all. And even though you clearly demonstrate your talents, you have a tough time putting a decent price tag on them.

We are not alone. Measuring your own market value is difficult for a lot of people, but women especially. Remember what the experts said: women get less because we expect less.

Journalists Claire Shipman and Katty Kay, authors of *The Confidence Code: The Art and Science of Self Assurance — What Women Should Know*, have found that no matter how competent women are, they still lack confidence.

That was the case even for some of the most successful women they talked with, like WNBA star Monique Currie and Clara Shih, the tech entrepreneur who founded Hearsay Social and joined the Starbucks board of directors at age 29. [21]

Crazy, right?

Writing in *The Atlantic*, Shipman and Kay say that, "Compared with men, women don't consider themselves as ready for promotions, they predict they'll do worse on tests, and they generally underestimate their abilities... Success, it turns out, correlates just as closely with confidence as it does with competence.[22]"

Research has also found that women tend to belittle our accomplishments, to explain away our success. In an article in *Redbook*, Colorado-based career and life coach Jenn DeWall said that because women are socialized to try to make others feel better, we don't want our success to make those around us feel bad about themselves.[23]

Valerie Young, Ed.D., author of *The Secret Thoughts of Successful Women*, adds, "I actually heard a woman say, 'If I can get a Ph.D. in astrophysics from Caltech, anyone can.[24]'"

Thinking back to when I first accepted my vice president position, I realize I was demonstrating those same tendencies.

I knew that when I was offered the vice president role, I would be low on the compensation scale. After all, I was a woman in my mid-thirties. I knew that others had turned down the job and that some leaders didn't think I was ready for it. I chose not to negotiate as I was extremly grateful that my future boss took a shot on me.

When it came time for my one-year performance review, the energy industry was in the midst of one of its worst cycles in decades. People were losing their jobs and construction was being scaled back. Making it clear that resources were limited, the company had committed to handing out very small wage increases. The leadership group would get their raises in stock instead of cash. Everyone's expectations were set and we were grateful to receive something greater than zero.

When my boss called to tell me about my raise, he said he had saved mine for last because he liked delivering good news. Oh, boy. Just like Christmas in his mind, I guess.

And the news was good: because I had, in his words, "exceeded anything the company thought [I] could do" (a back-handed compliment if ever there was one), I was getting a large — ok, a REALLY large — raise in both my base salary and bonus percentages. Actually, the raise was greater than the raise I got the year before when I made vice president.

You might be thinking, "Wow. That must mean a ton of money." Ha! I was thinking that, too, and maybe even starting to plan my next Nordstrom shopping trip. But then things started to sort of unfurl in my brain. It went something like this:

- Wow, that is a ton of money.

- Wow, this sure makes me feel compensated for all the hard work I put in this last year.

- Huh, wait a second. Didn't I just read that women are compensated for *performance* and men for *potential*? What, exactly, were the company's expectations of me? (Hit the replay button on the "exceeding anything the company thought [I] could do" comment.)

- Oh, no! I should have negotiated; I knew I should have negotiated. Why didn't I negotiate?

- Well I know why I didn't negotiate... I'm too scared to speak up. What if they withdrew the offer? "Would they have seen me as aggressive or ungrateful?"

- Wow, if you have that much to make up, I wonder if you're still underpaying me?

I knew that my original offer had been low, but I figured the company had at least made an attempt to be fair. I had assumed positive intent, figuring that they were still doing right by me.

As a woman in my mid-thirties, I knew that when I became a vice president, I would be low on the compensation scale. But it was only when the company tried to make up for it with a hefty raise that I realized how undervalued I had been. This has been a tremendous learning opportunity for me. The work world will always be full of slip-ups and disappointments, but how we deal with problems is what counts. In this case, I realized I had been undervalued in terms of both wages and expectations. But instead of quitting or throwing my arms up in self-defeat, I remained positive and proactive... and committed to getting better at negotiating.

Now, I saw that was not the case.

What made matters worse was that even though I was paid less than my predecessor, they had set high expectations for me. But what could I do? I couldn't say, "Hey, you're only paying me 65 percent as much as the previous guy, I'm going to only *achieve* 65 percent as much."

Companies can always find a reason to justify why they set salaries the way they do. They say that no two people are alike, and I know that's true. But I felt truly undervalued by this experience. And if I had mentioned it, I cannot even speculate what the response would have been.

Some time has passed now, and I've had some time to decide how I want to look at this. I was distressed and offended when I realized I was being underpaid, and I felt taken advantage of. But I refused — and refuse still — to let negative thinking take over and make my every day anything less than happy.

Instead, I've chosen to be grateful for what happened. It was a learning experience, and I used the knowledge I've gained productively. That is right, I negotiated my next offer with confidence. That is a sign of improvement right there.

Conversation Starters

What would it take for you to be comfortable negotiating a salary? If you already are: bravo! Send good vibes my way!

What is the worst excuse you've ever heard for denying a raise request?

Picturing Differences (On the Occasions When We Are Alike)

The term "corporate headshot" has long stirred fear in the heart of business leaders, and not just because it sounds like you're about to get a clunk to the brain rather than be photographed.

Unlike the holiday family picture, your last Snapchat selfie, or your wedding album, if you don't like your company portrait, you might not be able to escape it. It's a good bet that your picture will be displayed in some semi-public spot where you'll have to pass by it at least occasionally and wonder why you decided wearing that particular blouse with those earrings was a good idea in the first place. (And seriously — who figured it wasn't enough to show the head and shoulders and came up with the three-quarter length, problem area-baring stance? No wonder the Mona Lisa is smirking: she could keep her poochy tummy a secret.)

In my case, having a corporate photograph taken brought up an issue I had never anticipated — one that set me apart from my leadership group colleagues.

You see, our male executives all have a typical, conservative photo they're shown in dark suits positioned in front of one of those soft-focus backgrounds.

The communications team suggested something different for me: a more casual, on-the-job shot. Originally, I liked the idea. After all, I had asked for a second executive bio because I didn't think the traditional one accurately represented who I am as a leader and person.

But the execution of the headshot was, well, interesting. It was staged against an orange wall — making me look like a greeter at a big box store than the person responsible for 120 team members in a publicly held company with assets exceeding $7 billion.

What's more, it was taken with a camera phone by someone shorter than me. So I'm looking downward, which is not the most flattering angle for anyone.

Was I surprised by how extremely informal this photo shoot turned out to be? Yes. Did I know it was not going to produce the best picture? Yes. Was I reluctant to speak up? Yes. I did not want to hurt anyone's feelings by suggesting this was a bad idea. Of course, I also hoped that my portrait would be good enough so I wouldn't cringe every time I saw it. I also didn't want anyone else who had to pose for a headshot to have the same experience.

So after a lot of thought, rehearsing the conversation over and over in my head, I decided to speak up.

Although I wanted things to be different — let's face it, we were going to have to do a re-take — it was also important that the communications team knew how much I valued them, and that I counted on them to make things right. I calmly walked over to the communications department and asked for two things: could my picture be similar to the other leaders' portraits? And could someone be there on picture day to help me look my best?

And you know what? They didn't get defensive or try to make excuses. Instead, they were empathetic, agreeing the approach had not been successful. We worked out an easy solution, and they lined up hair and makeup for me. When the time came to take the photo, the communications team was there with me, selecting my outfit and helping me with poses. We had the best few hours together, and it strengthened our relationship. And the photo? It came out better than I could have imagined.

To this day, I'm still not sure why my first portrait session was planned the way it was. Maybe it was a compliment — perhaps they saw me as a different kind of leader and wanted to capture my youth and enthusiasm. You can't really find fault with intentions like that, especially when you've been branded the "fun" vice president. But this wasn't all about me or my "supermodel good looks." My hope was that by speaking up and addressing the issue in a calm, respectful way, things would be easier for the next person. And it has been: there was hair and makeup for the women *and* men who have been photographed since.

And no one had to stand against an orange wall.

I don't know why the communications department thought it would be a good idea to photograph me against an orange backdrop, unlike the other executives with their formal portraits. I didn't want to cause a scene or embarrass them, but I couldn't let it go, either. I wanted them to see that all of the leaders' pictures should be the same — and a little help with hair and makeup would be good for all of us, women and men alike. The fact is, women who express anger at work are perceived more negatively than men who exhibit the same behavior — men are just seen as assertive.

Conversation Starters

Are you comfortable being "the squeaky wheel" that gets the proverbial grease? If so, have you found that tactic effective?

Have you ever spoken out about an issue at work to "deaf ears"... only to see a male co-worker's similar gripe get resolved?

Making
Corporate
Culture Work
For You

We Talk, We Lead

CHAPTER 6: MAKING CORPORATE CULTURE WORK FOR YOU

During my career, I've worked for companies with very different cultures. At the Big Five accounting firm, for example, the culture was all about people and colleagues and teams that worked hard together — a great place to be if you have an outgoing personality like I do.

That didn't mean a more introverted personality couldn't get along there — in an accounting office, people who like numbers, organization, and detail don't have to look far to find a quiet, kindred spirit. But it might be a little stressful and take a fair amount of adjustment to live up to the organization's rah-rah philosophy.

That's one of the difficulties of "culture," I think: the company often demands that the person align with the culture, instead of the other way around. What I mean is, in a lot of companies, employees have to work hard, do more with less, put in longer hours, sacrifice family time — all to make the company (and its stakeholders) happy. But what does the company do to make the employee happy? That's often a short list.

As a leader, I have the opportunity to create a positive culture for my team. But my efforts can't be top down — it's not me deciding what the culture should be like. Instead, I have to listen to what my team members are telling me; I have to learn what they want the department to feel and be like. Then, I can use my authority to institute the changes that will make their culture come to life.

Getting to Yes

Corporate culture is composed of many important dimensions — vision, mission, values, people, and more — and it produces a lot of benefits. A strong culture helps companies attract and retain talent. It influences how successful the business becomes. And a weak culture? Well, fortunately, that can be changed.

When I became leader of the finance department, I walked into a culture that was perhaps best described as confused.

The finance leaders operated in silos, looking out for only their respective areas and merely co-existing. Quite frankly, this was not a team. My predecessor had left six months earlier, and the department was being monitored from afar, some 2,000 miles away at the corporate office, and the lack of oversight intensified the issues.

Almost from day one, what the leadership team wanted was for me to wave a magic wand and erase the past, to make everything right again in the blink of an eye.

Obviously, that was not a realistic expectation. It's impossible to make sweeping changes overnight. Instead, progress amounts to doing a lot of smaller things right over time (and learning when things go wrong first). At the start, it often felt like I was taking one step forward and 10 steps back. What kept me going was concentrating on that one step in the right direction.

I realized I could steady the course by listening to and observing the finance team.

It didn't take long for me to discover that the team was desperately seeking cooperation, loyalty, and trust. In other words, they wanted a new, collaborative culture, based on a sense of community, where individuals could thrive and feel energized.

But were we really ready to work toward that lofty goal together?

One way to find out was by actually working on a task together and, holding my first department "town hall" meeting seemed like the perfect opportunity. In my company, that's an opportunity for each department to get together a few times a year and discuss strategic priorities, review what's happening around the organization, and do some team development or training exercises.

Sadly, we almost didn't get past the meeting to *plan* the town hall.

I had gathered my finance leadership team with high hopes, thinking that in the hour ahead of us, I could provide the group with the information they would need to get the town hall off the ground. We'd knock out the town hall's big picture items — what the theme would be, the format, things like that — and leave with assignments and due dates in hand.

What do they say about best laid plans? Scrap them immediately?

Soon after we started, things fell into a predictable pattern: I would propose an idea, and my team members would tell me why it wouldn't work. We weren't even debating "real" stuff — the group couldn't agree on what we'd have for lunch. "Folks," I wanted to shout, "it's a small town, there aren't many options! Let's get together on this one, simple thing."

As you can imagine, the "it won't work" attitude really goes against my grain. I don't like hearing nay-sayers (even the ones inside my head).

I realize that I was asking the working group to look at things a new way — to join forces, cooperate, and be the cohesive group they said they'd wanted to be. That meant change, and it is human nature to resist change, even when it's for the better. Routine is often comforting and secure. New ideas and new ways of working can make us feel like we've lost our footing: what we'd thought of as "normal" doesn't really exist anymore. Even if the situation was negative, it was something we were used to.

Rosabeth Moss Kanter, writing in *Harvard Business Review*, suggests that in the workplace, people feel threatened by change not only because they fear losing control over their territory, but also because they fear "losing face.[25]" I can understand that — if the way you've been doing things is being tossed or updated because someone higher up the org chart sees it as ineffective, it's pretty easy to worry that you are somehow at fault or incompetent. Defending the old way of doing things comes naturally: how many times have you heard, "We've always done it that way so why would we change?" Even people who agree that with some adjustments, things could be accomplished more easily, can fall back on that phrase. I know I have.

For a department that indicated it wanted a cooperative culture, there were sure times when they didn't show it. During our pre-town hall planning session, the team members couldn't agree on anything, and the litany of "that won't work" comments began almost immediately. I have often wondered if the "it won't work" reflex is used simply as a mask and reflects a lack of trust. Instead of saying, "I don't like you/your idea/having to think about it/or the fact I will have to work harder," people find it easier to just say, "Nope. Won't work." Because I want to encourage honesty and teamwork, my answer is this: instead of saying it won't work, say, "Yes, it will." Then tell me what you need to make yes happen.

Clearly, this tendency to try to save face can keep us from moving forward. One way leaders can counter it, I've found, is to protect the dignity of team members during change. For me, that includes having them be part of determining the path forward, never saying the past was wrong, and using phrases such as, "I am sure that was the best decision at the time" (and meaning it).

Still, that doesn't always get us over the "it won't work" hump. What's been useful for me is this: I ask my team members to consider why something *will work* first. Because I believe that flat-out doing nothing is not an option, I've told my team that if you are asked to do something, the answer should be yes, assuming the request is not completely unreasonable. But then you have the right and the opportunity to describe the trade-offs or consequences of that request, such as resource support, budget dollars, or additional time. For example, it is absolutely acceptable for someone on my team to say "Yes, I can do that, but I'll need one extra person to help me for two weeks, which will mean taking Betsy off the project she's working on and delaying it." That lets me make a more informed decision about what the next steps should be.

What's more, my team members know that the same rules apply to me. When someone makes a request of me, I will almost always say yes first then ask for what I need to make yes happen.

I try to reserve saying no for the times when I really feel strongly about doing so, or for something that goes against the culture we are trying to create.

Like the time the finance senior leaders wanted to make using the huddle board concept mandatory for brainstorming sessions.

If you haven't heard of it, the huddle board method is increasingly popular for team building and problem solving. Typically, the group gathers for about 15 minutes to discuss issues, opportunities, and solutions. In most cases, everything is tracked on a whiteboard or similar physical device.

The thing is, for some people, this isn't the most productive or creative way to work. Because I believe the best approach is to let each team decide which brainstorming concept works best for them, I could never mandate a one-size-fits-all process. At the same time, I didn't just want to flat-out say no to my finance senior leaders. Instead, I decided to guide them to what I thought was the right solution.

I began by asking questions, such as:

1. Why did we want to introduce the huddle board?

2. If it does not work for everyone, will we want them to keep using it?

3. How much creative license would the individuals have?

Eventually, the finance senior leaders came to the conclusion I had hoped they would. They backed away from their decision to force everyone to use the huddle board. Everyone felt the right decision had been made — and I hadn't had to say "no."

Our "say yes first" attitude has become an important part of the finance department's improved culture. We understand better how to work with one another as members of a cohesive team, and that's given us a lot of wins. We manage our expectations, support one another, and are genuinely happy together. When I joined the department, no one knew what our vision statement was. Now, we all have it memorized. People who visit us say they can feel the energy we exude. The biggest compliment about our healthy culture is probably the fact that talented people from other areas of the company are eager to transfer into our department. We've even heard people say, 'Finance is the place to be.'

Time has passed and that magic wand still hasn't appeared in my hand. But working with my team to create the kind of culture they always wanted — one that is anything but confused — has been a pretty charmed experience.

Wendy's Way to Success: Creativity is Key

I was contemplating what a good team-building activity might be when it hit me: with Easter just a few weeks away, how about an egg hunt on the Thursday before the holiday? We'd call it a spring celebration so everyone would feel included, and it would give the team members something to do together, helping to create the energy and culture of community they said they wanted.

I ran the idea past my leadership team. They responded with such shock and horror you would have thought I had kidnapped the Easter Bunny or eaten all the Peeps.

"You can't do it on that day," they cried. "That's right when we're closing the books for the quarter, and most people don't want to be disturbed!"

Granted, that made some sense. But to me, this was a stressful period where getting a break and having a little fun would lift spirits and energize the group for the long haul ahead.

A common technique I use when planning something unusual is to ask myself, "What is the worst-case scenario, and how would I recover?" If I can live with that answer, then I proceed full steam ahead.

So, unsure if anyone would participate, I went forth with my plan. I told my team members they could decorate their work areas if they wanted and recruited some of their kids to hide the eggs — including several golden eggs that could be redeemed for prizes.

The day of the event, our department looked like a pastel wonderland. Each pod — an area for six to eight team members with cubicles around the perimeter and a small conference table in the middle — was outfitted with a distinct theme.

Many team members arrived at work in spring colors; still others brought baskets for egg collecting. Someone took a photo of the group on the hunt, which another team member had enlarged and framed for our department's future memorabilia case.

It didn't take long for all the eggs to be tracked down (well, except for a couple that we had hidden too well, but we had fun searching for them, too) and soon, everyone was back at work. And you know what? No deadlines were missed in the making of a stronger culture.

Conversation Starters

How will you know when you're in the right culture?

What is your strategy when faced with the "that won't work" (or the, "we've always done it this way") mentality?

Could you apply my "say yes first" strategy to encourage team members to consider why something will work before discussing the drawbacks?

Don't Put Your Personality in a Drawer

Clearly, I feel it has been a privilege and pleasure to take the lead in creating a culture where my team can flourish.

Culture is a complex system, and it has a lot of moving parts. That includes big-picture items like values, vision, and mission, as well as day-to-day activities, such as how people communicate and get along with one another. Human resources expert Susan M. Heathfield says,

"Culture is the environment that surrounds you at work all of the time. Culture is a powerful element that shapes your work enjoyment, your work relationships, and your work processes... Culture is the behavior that results when a group arrives at a set of — generally unspoken and unwritten — rules for working together.[26]"

I'm glad to say that my team members work well within the corporate culture we've built. But sometimes, people talk about being forced to *conform to* the culture, instead.

What is the difference?

To me, working within a culture means that our values and the company's values are in sync *and* we're allowed to let our personality shine. In other words, *how* the work gets done is less important than the fact *that* it gets done — as long as customers and other stakeholders are happy and business goals are met.

As you might imagine, these are the environments where staff members feel comfortable, are excited to come to work, and are focused on helping one another achieve common goals.

When I was at the Big Five accounting company, the culture was all about relationships: the people who you knew and hung out with. As a gregarious person, this culture was a good fit for me, and I knew I could work within it. I quickly realized that to be successful, I needed to be part of a large circle of colleagues. I roomed with a woman from the same company and to this day, some of my best friends are people I met on the job.

But what about the flip side, being pushed to *conform* to culture that isn't a good fit for us? William Arruda writes in *Forbes* that can mean masking who we are, leaving our true selves at the office door, and not making too many waves.[27]

Doesn't sound like me, does it? And it isn't what I want for my team, either. The thing is, a lot of companies — large, successful ones, too — expect conformance. That can make working life a drag. No one wants to wake up dreading what is ahead of them at the office, which is why trying to conform to a culture that we're not suited for has been linked to depression, loss of productivity, and a lack of loyalty.

How bad can it get? I once read about a company that prided itself so much on its hard-working culture that it actually boasted about making a bride come into the office on her wedding day!

And while I've never been part of an organization quite like that, when I worked for the airline, I did have a negative run-in with corporate culture.

It was just a little bulletin board with plane ticket stubs on it, meant to help me remember the trips I'd taken since joining the airline. It made me appreciate the company for its employee perks and motivated me to work even harder. But instead of seeing it that way, my boss thought it meant I was taking too much time off. And even though my productivity made my work ethic clear, he thought the perception would exist as long as the tickets were on display, and so, I took them down. I decided that I would never ask my team members to conform to a culture that isn't good for them. Instead, I'd find ways to create a culture that works for us. In my current job, in fact, I have a bulletin board that is filled with photos of our team. It reminds us of the successes we've had together.

As I've mentioned, one of the advantages of being in the travel industry is, no surprise, getting to travel — typically for free or at least drastically reduced rates. For front-line people like flight attendants and gate agents, there's no question that getting a free trip can go a long way toward making up for extensive hours and having to deal with difficult or unruly customers.

Of course, those same benefits are available at the corporate level, for people like accountants who never have to come face-to-face with a crying, airsick child (other than their own), or an overstressed, belligerent adult.

I love to travel, and I am sentimental about my journeys. So, to me, it only made sense that, as an airline employee, I'd keep a little bulletin board collection of ticket stubs. Not only did it help me remember my trips, I thought it showed my loyalty. You know, like putting up college pennants in your dorm room.

What I hadn't anticipated was how my boss might perceive the display. Instead of seeing it for what it was — my way to preserve memories — he thought that it was a slight against our nose-to-the-grindstone culture. He called me into his office to ask me, point-blank, if I was taking too much vacation.

My response was measured. I told him that the next day, I'd provide a calendar that showed that I had not been out too much.

But even after looking at the dates I'd been gone, he still wasn't satisfied. He said the perception that I was burning through time off would remain as long as my ticket stubs were on view.

I conformed to culture and took them down. I didn't stop traveling, but I did stop discussing my trips with my co-workers. I became closed off. I lost trust in others.

My memories were no longer appropriate for the office. I'd had to put a little piece of my personality in a drawer.

It was incidents like this one that were on my mind when I joined the finance department at my current company. I was determined that my team members wouldn't have to conform to whatever new culture we established, but that they would be allowed, instead, to work within it. I would help them learn, understand, and identify with our department's vision and goals. I would encourage collaboration and cohesion, but they would have the freedom to be themselves, and to be productive in their own ways.

As an example to them, I decided to repurpose one of our small conference rooms into a more comfortable space, like a lounge or living room. The reason? Being in a colorful, comfortable space encourages some of my best thinking. And when I'm in a rut, different surroundings can help me see things, well, differently. Being able to get out from behind a desk and into a less rigid setting works wonders for me, and it has for many of my team members, too.

Our culture isn't just about sitting in a living room-like setting, of course. Fitness challenges have also played a big part in our cultural evolution. While you might think with my tennis background I would be all over this, I don't necessarily see the need to take a month to build up to 100 pushups in a day. However, there is a small group of folks in the finance department who started these challenges, and they *love* them. Through their encouragement, participation has grown to the point that the entire department is involved. So yes, I will be doing 100 pushups on the last day of the current challenge.

Conversation Starters

Have you been forced to conform to a culture that isn't good for you?

What do you do to maintain your authentic self in the workplace?

Building Trust, One-on-One, One-by-One

Little walks and little talks. Iced tea and bunny ears.

They may seem like small things, but being spontaneous and lighthearted is really a big part of who I am as a person and as a leader. Impromptu conversations have allowed me to create personal connections with the people I work with. And when my team members see the real me — silly get-ups and all — they feel comfortable letting me know who they are, too.

I'm not suggesting that co-workers engage in an oversharing free-for-all. We don't need to know every last detail about one another. (And isn't that what social media is for, anyway?)

I have found, however, that feeling connected to one another helps us build trust, which is a pretty big deal in the workplace. Trust is vital to communication, collaboration, teamwork, and performance — all factors that increase the likelihood of our being successful together. In essence, trust is essential to a positive culture.

On the flip side, when co-workers distrust one another, it can make for an unhealthy office environment. When people doubt that others have their best interests at heart, communication and collaboration can collapse. The next to go is productivity. After all, it's pretty hard to get things done when you're always looking over your shoulder.

None of this is exactly news: establishing trust has long been proven to be a core competency for a leader. But how do you make it real? Here's how I went about it.

When I joined the finance department, I couldn't assume that people would automatically place their trust in me. But I knew that to be able to accomplish what we needed to as a group, building trust was essential, and it was my responsibility. I couldn't assume that people automatically trusted me because I was their boss.

So I worked at doing the kinds of things that showed my team members I sought and valued their confidence in me. That included:

- Being honest and open in my interactions with my team members, including having the hard conversations.

- Listening to others' ideas and confirming I have faith in my team members' decision making.

- Focusing on progress, not perfection, and helping people build on their strengths.

- Acknowledging my team members' feelings and opinions; treating each person as an individual with unique needs and talents.

That last bullet point — treating each person as the unique individual he or she is — can be troublesome for some leaders. It's not easy, for example, when you have been taught or conditioned to stick strictly to issues in the workplace and ignore the fact that personalities are involved. And it can be a roadblock for leaders who are inclined to take a cookie-cutter approach with their team members that regards people as indistinguishable from one another.

But the thing is, when people come to work, they don't check their personalities at the door. How many times have you heard, "It's just business; don't take it personally"? That drives me crazy because, *of course* it's personal. We don't stop being the people we are when we come into the office. Hard workers are still hard workers; optimists still have a sunny outlook, even when tough deadlines bear down on them; thin-skinned individuals can get their feelings hurt at the slightest, even well-intentioned remark. By removing personality from the equation, I think you limit the possibility of understanding one another. It is easy to make false assumptions about how to get along and what it will take to solve problems in a way where everyone wins. I say learn from situations, take them personally, and personally become better for it.

Here's an example of what I mean. One time, a group of us had gathered for what I like to call a "solutions session." That's a positive way of saying we're going to explore issues in our division and figure out what we'll do about them.

As we were hashing out a problem, the meeting switched gears unexpectedly. Going south might be a polite way of saying it.

One woman who reports to me — who I think is amazing and respect a lot — basically shut down.

You know how sometimes people who are stewing and filled with resentment will continue to put on a happy face, blindsiding you later? This was not one of those occasions. From her body language and facial expression, her displeasure was clear. She might not have been ready to say something, but she was sure being honest with her emotions otherwise. Maybe she'd flashed back to the way the department was before I joined it. I know those weren't exactly the good old days.

Building trust is a multi-faceted process that's essential to getting along and being productive. When colleagues trust one another, there's harmony in the workplace. But getting everyone in the right key isn't always easy. We don't check our personalities at the door when we get to the office, and that means different types of people with different styles of working somehow have to blend. How can we help this along? I think the first step is getting out and getting to know who we're working with. It's the only way we can fully understand the talents, experience, concerns, and quirks that everyone brings to the table. That helps us tailor the way we act and how we behave so we can create strong relationships and overcome problems with less effort.

I'm a pretty intuitive person. I can usually tell when there's a disturbance in the Force. But this time was different: a team member was signaling that something had gone seriously awry.

What could I do? Someone else might not have minded me asking, "What's wrong?" or "Do you want to say something?" In this case, though, I knew that would have only made things worse.

So I did what I thought was best: I continued on. I trusted that she would process what was bothering her and come back to me.

Sure enough, about two hours later, she came into my office and said: "That did not go well."

Then, she added, "Let's talk about it." True music to my ears. I resisted every urge to stand up and give her a hug. (It should come as little surprise that I'm a big hugger.)

We had a great discussion, hashed out a lot of issues, and parted optimistic about making things better.

I was grateful that she trusted me to speak frankly to me. I was also grateful that she trusted me to listen and help sort things out. Our relationship is stronger for it. Equally important, our team is stronger for it.

Could this have happened on Day One, when I began leading the finance department? Of course not. You can't walk in and immediately think you know people. What worked in this instance might have been the absolute worst approach with another team member. But I never could have known that at the start.

But this is more than getting to know the people I work with: it's about letting them know me, too. My team members have a realistic sense of who I truly am, and what I'm really like. The benefit of this transparency is that my team member knew my door would be open when she was ready to talk, and that we could have a forthright and meaningful conversation. But what if she hadn't seen that as an option? She might have become disruptive, igniting the people around her. Chaos could have been just one comment away.

The workplace that allows us to be our best selves is a workplace that functions smoothly and well. By taking little steps to open yourself to others and getting to know them — one-on-one, one by one — you can build that kind of environment... and build big trust along the way.

Conversation Starters

What are steps you take to get new colleagues to trust you?

**What is the number one reason why you would
lose trust in a co-worker?**

**I was confident my direct report would come to me after the
meeting. But if you'd been in my shoes, how would you have
handled the situation if she hadn't shown up?**

Of Mothers
and Mentors

We Talk, We Lead

CHAPTER 7: OF MOTHERS AND MENTORS

The African proverb "It takes a village to raise a child," is often used to express the kinds of partnerships required to nurture a person from infancy to adulthood.

I've found that the same kind of help and encouragement is welcome, important, and maybe even required for everyone in the work world. To progress in the right direction and achieve our goals, we need all kinds of support.

Sometimes, that assistance comes in the form of an official mentoring relationship, with a more experienced person providing professional guidance. Other times, it's a best friend giving you a symbolic slap upside the head and telling you to fly right. For me, mentors have come in many different forms. Some have even seemed a little like parents, without the judgment and curfews.

My mentors have made a very real difference in my work life. And because I've seen how important these relationships can be, I've been happy to mentor others. As a result, I've learned that mentoring isn't a one-way street so much as a mutually beneficial experience. Being a mentor has helped me improve my self-awareness and connections to others. And it's very satisfying to think that, at least in some part, I've helped other people flourish.

Of course, I like to think that, to some degree, I strive to mentor nearly everyone in the finance department. One way I do that is by recognizing that each individual needs validation in a different way. For the team member who needs to feel heard, I set aside extra time for our meetings. I never want her to feel rushed.

Another team member needs to know that the work she is doing is being used. I make a point of circling back with her after meetings or presentations to let her know how she contributed, if it wasn't already apparent.

One person likes to attend or represent finance in special conferences or events. I recognize that he is also much better at some of the provincial political outings than I am, so I have him attend on my behalf. He loves that.

My newest team member just needs space to try things and develop his own leadership style. I try to say "yes" or "great idea" as much as possible. And when something does not go as planned, I try to make sure he realizes this is all part of the journey.

Many Voices, Much Support

Throughout my career, a variety of diverse and incredible people have mentored me in important ways. Sometimes, it was part of a formal, professional arrangement; others were on a more casual basis.

Regardless of how the relationship was established or how long it lasted, each one was valuable and contributed to my journey and my accomplishments.

Although I can't adequately describe here how each person added to my professional life (and even to my personal life, in varying degrees), I know I'm better for having been guided or counseled by each of them. Granted, some of them don't fit the classic definition of a mentor; others may not have even realized they were mentoring me. But each played an important role in my development as a leader. At one time or another, I needed their wisdom, direction, and advice, and I benefited tremendously every time they generously provided those things. Consider the variety of mentors I've had:

1. There was the technical accounting guru, who would engage me in a riveting discussion, complete with flow charts and decision trees, no matter what unusual transaction I was dealing with.

2. My office politics genius, who would always know the right person to ask in order to move work forward… or get the newest office chair.

3. My office "high school best friend" — who shoots it to me straight and doesn't mince words, especially when it comes to reflecting on my own reactions.

4. Inspirational mentors, who ask those tough questions that leave you speechless and keep you up at night thinking, and who give you the energy to keep striving for your goals.

5. My "devil's advocate," who will challenge me every step of the way, until we finally reach a compromise which proves to me a magical solution.

6. The MBA professor who helped me focus in on my passion and bridge the theoretical with the practical.

7. My go-to external consultant that after years of working together from the trenches to leadership positions, his advice and trusting friendship is where I turn to during difficult times.

Oh, yes, and even a formal, company-appointed mentor.

If it seems like that's an awful lot of people for one woman to turn to for support, well, that's not even close to all of them. Today's world and workplace are complex and constantly changing, and, it would be great if there were just one person who could give you all the coaching you would need over your 40+ year career. But I can't even imagine having all of the skills it would take to fill that role, much less the stamina.

In recent years, one relationship stands out, and that's the one I have with Laura. She was an executive who was senior to me when we met, and I still look up to her today.

Laura and I never set up a formal mentoring agreement; our

friendship developed naturally. I give her credit for helping me the most when it comes to finding an equilibrium between work and life.

One example of her keen abilities to teach me this tricky balancing act dates back several years, to the time soon after I returned to work following my three-month maternity leave.

With the birth of my son, my entire life had just been turned upside down in an amazing, wonderful way. I had a new, extremely important job and a very short title to go with it: Mom. And being a mom was now my priority.

I've had a lot of mentors, and I've been a mentor, too. The more people you have in your life who can coach you, support you, and advocate on your behalf, the better. The best mentors will know you so well that they can identify your needs as easily — or even better — than you can. Wherever you are in your career journey, I recommend being a mentor if you have the opportunity. As a mentor, you'll get to fine-tune your communication skills, be seen as a leader, and recognize how far you've come in your own career. More than that, you'll learn. Trust me: there will be plenty of times when the student will become the master, helping you discover new ways of interpreting situations, approaching problems, and developing solutions.

Motherhood made me feel like a completely different person in some ways. I'd always been adept at taking care of myself, but now I had someone else to be responsible for. My son's happiness and security were the first things I thought of when I woke up, and they were never far from my mind the rest of the day. But let on at the office that something else other than work was occupying my mind? No way would I allow that to happen. I didn't want to be perceived as anyone but the high-spirited, team-building, diligent worker I'd always been.

So I did what I thought was best: I jumped back in, 150 percent (yes, as an accountant, I realize that's a statistical impossibility. It does, however, reflect my level of effort and how I wanted to be perceived). I brought forward a new technology solution, volunteered to organize charitable giving projects, and was still working towards my MBA. See? I was trying to say, "I've been gone, now I am back, and I didn't miss a beat. I'm Workplace Wendy, the one you've always known and depended on."

I was walking down the hallway, arms full of binders, when I ran into Laura. We took a minute to greet each other and catch up — as much as we could, anyway, while heading toward appointments in opposite directions.

Before she said good-bye, though, Laura became very serious. She looked me straight in the eye with the kind of care and concern we often associate with our mothers, only without the part where we feel like a child.

"You have been off for three months," she said, "which means you need to give yourself at least that much time to get back to full strength."

I stood there thunderstruck.

I hadn't said I was tired or struggling or anything but skipping through my workday as carefree as could be.

Yet, because of our trusting "mentoring" relationship, she could identify my needs without being told what they were. At the same time, I was open to hearing her opinion and advice because she'd counseled me so well in the past. It was in that moment that I realized how priceless mentoring can be and what a great impact the connections between mentors and mentees can have.

The thing is, Laura might not have even realized the huge gift her words were to me or how this one exchange had such a profound and pivotal impact on me. I saw a real leader in action, someone who genuinely cares. Someone I genuinely work to be like. And the fact is, her advice has rippled out to many others — I've shared her words with many new moms, and they all seemed grateful to hear it.

Now that I'm an executive, I think back on the impact Laura and so many others have had on me. Whatever you call the people who provide guidance and support — mentor, sponsor, counselor, coach, or even a "high school best friend" at the office — I've found you can't have enough of these individuals in your life. And embracing their insights can have a huge impact on your work life and career.

Conversation Starters

Think of the mentors, advisors, or confidants in your life. How have they helped you?

What is your favorite attribute of a mentor?

Have you fulfilled any of those roles for someone else? Did that person ever tell you what you meant to them?

What Gender is Your Mentor (and Does It Matter)?

Mentoring relationships can be formal or casual, life-changing or short-lived, deeply emotional, or highly superficial.

One thing that seems to be in question is whether they can be mixed-gender.

Yes, even in our highly enlightened age, many men and women still have qualms about mentoring someone of the opposite sex.

Some women say that only another woman can truly understand what their workplace issues are. But as Roy Cohen, author of *The Wall Street Professional's Survival Guide*, notes, there simply aren't sufficient female mentors to go around.

"It is a practical matter," Cohen was quoted on The Glass Hammer, an online career resource for professional women. "There are just not enough women in leadership positions, and like any community, not all of them want to, or can, be mentors. For those who do, they tend to be burdened by requests from many, many women—too many.[28]"

Adam reached out to me to mentor him precisely because I'm a woman and a mother, and I could anticipate the kind of issues he'd face as a new dad. Over time, I've realized that mentoring and mothering have a lot in common: you nurture, you watch for growth, and sometimes you have to dole out some tough love, like making sure your mentee is open to new ideas and is accountable for his or her part of the relationship. I've found, though, that when people trust you have their best interests in mind, they will take your input and suggestions to heart.

The shortage of female mentors aside, being limited by gender reduces the potential pool of ideal mentors by 50 percent. Your perfect match might be the one you wouldn't even consider.

When it came time for him to pick a mentor, my colleague Adam not only bucked the no-opposite-sex trend, he reached out to me specifically *because* I am a woman, wife, and mother.

When he asked me to consider a six-month mentoring relationship, Adam's wife was pregnant and he was contemplating taking a new position in our organization. But he worried that if he did, no one would remember that he was the father of a newborn. What if he were expected to agree without hesitation to late nights, travel, and other situations that would keep him from providing the support he knew his wife would need? He told me my perspective would help him balance family life with his prospective work requirements.

Brilliant! So very thoughtful. And very difficult for me to resist. How could I say no?

At this time in his career and life, I was the exact, right mentor for Adam. My gender *did* make a difference — in a completely positive way. As a woman who understands the pressures of "working while parenting," I could deliver advice (without any of the guilt) that would help him keep his family his priority while still stepping up to meet — even exceed — his job responsibilities.

Obviously, there's a line between mentoring and mothering. But in a very real sense, mentoring isn't all that different from raising children: you're nurturing others, advocating on their behalf, and encouraging them to grow and learn. But sometimes you have to give them the freedom to fall down, scrape their knees, and get back up on their own. Just like mom, right? Am I suggesting you treat the other person as if he or she is a child? Not any more than I'm suggesting you wipe off your co-workers' mouth after lunch.

But I am saying that the feminine or mothering instincts most women bring to the workplace do, indeed, belong there, and that those qualities make us good mentors, regardless of the mentee's gender.

Conversation Starters

Have you ever talked yourself out of a potentially valuable mentoring relationship because the person didn't fit your ideal mold?

Does gender play a role when you're making decisions about who your mentors will be?

Sound Off: Tooting Your Own Horn, If Only to Yourself

One of the great things about mentorship is knowing there is someone who will put a yardstick against your performance and measure how much you've grown. No matter how confident or competent we feel, it's nice to hear validation from someone outside of our annual performance appraisal. Even the accomplished, generally assured executives in my company have expressed self-doubt to me. They say they simply can't gauge how well they do during presentations or speeches and need my honest appraisal. As for me, even though you know I don't put a lot of stock in fawning compliments, I still require others' feedback so I can be sure I'm on the right track.

(And on those days when we're feeling less sure of ourselves, positive comments can be as mood-boosting as savoring your recommended daily 1.4-ounce portion of dark chocolate — which has been scientifically proven to reduce stress hormones, in case you need another reason to keep some Godiva in your desk.)[29]

Listening to encouraging external voices is great, sure, but even the most attentive mentor won't be there to give you a daily affirmation. Sometimes, you just have to tell yourself that you've made a difference. Be willing to pat yourself on the back. Yes, I realize that's a tough one: most women I know are hesitant to recognize their own accomplishments. Self-deprecation — you know, like "Cal Tech aerospace can't be that great if they'd give me a Ph.D." — is a feminine trait. There is plenty of evidence out there, from blogs to major publications to scholarly research, suggesting that women simply aren't comfortable tooting their own horns, not even to ourselves. Nope, we have a hard time mustering even the tiny little bleat of a paper party horn. Or, as writer Whitney Johnson says, "Nice girls don't ask for praise, even from themselves."

One reason for this, Johnson claims, is gender bias: women have been conditioned to avoid being what might be thought of as self-aggrandizing — only in it for themselves, an egomaniac, stuck up. In the *Harvard Business Review*, Johnson cites an example from her own career of what happened when she tried to take the credit she was due:

> [W]e've observed men effectively use the royal 'we' to flag their accomplishments, earning plaudits for being gracious, and their leadership is never disputed. When a woman speaks in terms of 'we,' the accolades often get attributed to or co-opted by the entire team, with observers wondering if she even brought any skills to the task, other than an ability to delegate... I remember one particular conversation with a former boss. After seeing my accomplishments perpetually co-opted, I explicitly outlined for him what I had achieved for our firm. His response: "Why are you so self-promoting? Can't you just do the work and not talk about it?[30]"

I'm not sure exactly what my response would have been to a comment like that, but, without a doubt, he would be *my* former boss, too.

Johnson offers a few ways we can work to overcome our reluctance to self-praise. Some of them are more public like including yourself when you name everyone who contributed to a success. Others (like today's *second* piece of dark chocolate) are for private consumption only: for example, jotting down your successes in a notebook (or, I suppose, on the back of a candy wrapper) or posting them as a note on your smartphone.

I've come up with a simple approach — a sort of self-mentoring — that reminds me I've made a difference since becoming head of the finance department. It might work for you, too.

Most people don't like to be seen as stuck-up or egomaniacs. But engaging in a little self-praise is like being your own mentor. My bulletin board of photos and memorabilia from my team's events and successes helps me remember why I'm here — and helps me celebrate what we've already accomplished. At the same time, it's motivating. Although I am not the kind of person to rest on my laurels anyway, seeing these happy faces makes me want to work even harder, to keep the team moving in the right direction and achieving even more.

You'll remember that it didn't take long for me to realize that my team members were yearning for a culture of community. I've worked diligently to build community in many ways, including organizing events that foster camaraderie and partnership but also have an element of fun. Among them: an Easter egg hunt, Ugly Sweater Day, cheering on another executive who was chosen for the dunk tank during a United Way fundraiser, and the two consecutive campaigns when we won the Golden Backpack Award for donating the most school supplies in a company-wide drive.

I have saved photos and mementos from each of those events and display them in my office (actually, I'm looking for a more communal space where all of the team can enjoy them). When I glance over and see Sara beaming with her basket of plastic eggs or Theresa and Warren triumphantly hoisting a gilded backpack over their heads, I know that my team members feel happy and fulfilled at work, that we are a close-knit bunch who support each other, and that we've all come a long way together from the drastically different culture of the finance department before I got here. I'm not in most of the photos; I have no great desire to see that much of myself and it's not about me, anyway. But those pictures are a small, subtle reminder of why I am here and why I deserve to recognize my accomplishments.

I also save thank you notes and I've started collecting motivational phrases — you wouldn't believe where I find some of the best ones, like on shopping bags. That reminds me to always keep my eyes open as I never know what I will find.

Maybe you have some mementos of your own that you can tack on your bulletin board, things that remind you of your professional victories. What about the note of appreciation from a co-worker or the invitation to attend a seminar that only a select few in your group received? Giving yourself credit is difficult, I know, but little tricks like a display or scrapbook will help you see for yourself that you are capable and competent. And that builds your self-confidence, which can ultimately benefit your company.

Wendy's Way to Success: Ask the Right Questions

As both a one-on-one mentor and the leader of large numbers of people, I've learned that certain conversations — performance appraisals and such — can be awkward and difficult. It's no fun having to tell someone they've fallen short, especially when that person has generally been a top-notch performer.

I've read all the hints and tips — start with the positive, be specific, talk about the work rather than the individual — but the suggestion most useful to me is to remember that my comments should be worded to help the other person grow. This is so important I am going to repeat it: the performance evaluation is about the other person... not me. My remarks are not intended to make me feel happy or good about myself. Yes, I like to be nice. But I have to be honest. That includes being up-front about what my concerns are, outlining my expectations, and offering possible solutions — while still giving the mentee or team member the freedom and support to solve the issues in his or her own way. At the end of the day, what we're after is a shared plan for improvement.

One strategy that has been particularly successful for me is asking questions that help me better understand the point of view of the person receiving my feedback. Did they lack the tools they needed? Was there something going on outside of office hours that was interfering with their productivity? Did I contribute to their problem in some way? Encouraging this kind of discussion can keep the mentee or team member from feeling hurt, defensive, or unwilling to respond. Beyond that, it provides a chance for them to self-evaluate, to get to that ah-ha moment that unlocks the past and paves the way for a more productive future. And if I should sense that things are going downhill, I've created a safe situation where I can say, "Reflecting on our conversation, I have the impression you're confused, irritated, or angry. How can we resolve that before *going on?" (You know what? This process keeps me from getting defensive, too. Because the focus is on making things better, I can trust that anything the other person says about me is intended in that spirit — not as a personal attack.)*

While I've used this technique for formal appraisals, it works equally well when the time comes to deliver more casual feedback. Whether you're at the top level of your company or want to share some constructive thoughts with the person on the other side of the cubicle from you, it's an effective approach.

Conversation Starters

Toot your own horn: what's your greatest accomplishment?

Pat yourself on the back:
how did it prepare you for the next step in your career?

Sing your own praises: where are you going from here?

EPILOGUE

My anthem, "This One's for the Girls" by Martina McBride, blares on the radio.

I sit at the kitchen island with a laptop, an iced tea, and a lemon square, trying to find the right words to wrap up this book.

My attention is suddenly captivated, as my eyes fixate on my two friends bouncing their baby girls on their hips while helping me make this book a reality. Our priorities shift, brainstorming the book ending fades into the background, and we start to talk.

How will work change when a friend returns from maternity leave? How will she balance the demands of raising a family and pursuing a career? Will she miss an important work opportunity because she had to stay home to look after a sick kid? We talk about everything from my friends' first day back at work to hopes for their daughters.

And while the perfect words to capture an ending elude me, this picture-perfect moment does not. Rather than an epilogue, this could be a prologue.

We all have stories. Women helping women. Women pushing boundaries and speaking up. Women who overcome adversity and challenges. Our stories can be about different experiences that happen in the smallest moments of our day or those that feel like major life-defining moments.

When I started this journey, my purpose was simple. I wanted my stories to be the catalyst to start meaningful conversations with other women. Conversations about mentoring, negotiating, finding your balance, and being your authentic self. We all hear about these challenges in the media every day, and we can relate. But where can we start? My answer is simple.

Just talk. Initiate the conversation, whether you use one of the questions in my book or have some of your own. Grab a tall glass of iced tea, take a sip, and start talking.

Just. Take. That. First. Step.

I did it. You can do it, too, because when *We Talk, We Lead.*

ACKNOWLEDGMENTS

Writing a book is scary and fun and nerve-racking and exciting.
At many times over the two-year process, it would have been
so much easier to just throw in the towel. I am forever grateful
for those friends, family and colleagues who kept me going.
I would not have finished without y'all.

Follow me on Instagram @wendyzelond

NOTES

1. " Facts About Arnold Glasgow," FixQuotes.com, accessed June 7, 2016, http://fixquotes.com/authors/arnold-h-glasgow.htm.

2. Chrissy Scivicque, "4 Reasons to Share Credit with Your Team," Ivy Exec, http://www.ivyexec.com/executive-insights/2016/share-credit-with-your-team.

3. Rebecca Nicholson, "Mindy Kaling: 'I wasn't considered attractive or funny enough to play myself,'" *The Guardian,* June 1, 2014, http://www.theguardian.com/tv-and-radio/2014/jun/01/mindy-kaling-project.

4. Tris Thorp, "How to Set Healthy Relationship Boundaries," The Chopra Center, accessed May 9, 2016, http://chopra.com/articles/how-to-set-healthy-relationship-boundaries.

5. Michelle Martin, "Learning to Trust Your Women's Intuition," *Huffington Post Canada,* June 7, 2017, http://www.huffingtonpost.com/michelle-martin/womens-intuition_b_10192222.html.

6. John Kreiser, "Bush: The Decider-in-Chief," *CBS News*, April 20, 2006, http://www.cbsnews.com/news/bush-the-decider-in-chief.

7. The Decider," The Urban Dictionary, accessed September 21, 2016, http://www.urbandictionary.com/define.php?term=The%20Decider.

8. Kari Reston, "Should You Apply for a Job You're Not Qualified For?" *The Muse*, accessed July 12, 2016, http://www.themuse.com/advice/should-you-apply-for-a-job-youre-not-qualified-for.

9. Suzanne Gerber, "Why Even Strong Women Sometimes Have a Hard Time Saying No," *Next Avenue*, February 29, 2012, http://www.nextavenue.org/why-even-strong-women-sometimes-have-hard-time-saying-no.

10. Nigel Marsh, "How to Make Work-Life Balance Work," *TEDxSydney*, May 2010, http://www.ted.com/talks/nigel_marsh_how_to_make_work_life_balance_work.

11. "Labor force participation rate, female," Report, World Bank, March 2017, http://www.worldbank.org/content/dam/Worldbank/document/Gender/GenderAtWork_web.pdf.

12. Olga Khazan, "America's Deep Rift on Gender Issues," *The Atlantic*, December 15, 2017, http://www.theatlantic.com/science/archive/2017/12/pew-gender/547508.

13. Simone Milasas, "Do You Do Business Like a Man Or a Woman?" *Inside Small Business*, August 4, 2014, http://insidesmallbusiness.com.au/planning-management/business-like-man-woman.

14. Gail Evans, "Play Like a Man, Win Like a Woman: What Men Know About Success That Women Need to Learn," (Crown Business, 2001).

15. Michael Michalowicz, "8 Traits Every Male Leader Needs to Learn from Women," American Express, accessed October 18, 2016, http://www.americanexpress.com/us/small-business/openforum/articles/8-traits-every-male-leader-needs-to-learn-from-women/.

16. Carol Toller, "New research shows women execs really do think differently – that's why we need more," *Canadian Business*, May 7, 2013, http://www.canadianbusiness.com/companies-and-industries/different-can-mean-better/.

17. Olga Khazan, "Women Know When Negotiating Isn't Worth It," *The Atlantic*, January 6, 2017, http://www.theatlantic.com/business/archive/2017/01/women-negotiating/512174.

18. " Women and Negotiation: Are There Really Gender Differences?" Knowledge@Wharton, The Wharton School, University of Pennsylvania, October 26, 2015, http://knowledge.wharton.upenn.edu/article/women-and-negotiation-are-there-really-gender-differences.

19. Linda Babcock and Sara Laschever, "Women Don't Ask: The High Cost of Avoiding Negotiation — and Positive Strategies for Change," (Bantam, 2007).

20. Maria Konnikova, "Lean Out: The Dangers for Women Who Negotiate," *The New Yorker*, June 10, 2014, http://www.newyorker.com/science/maria-konnikova/lean-out-the-dangers-for-women-who-negotiate.

21. Katty Kay and Claire Shipman, "The Confidence Code: The Science and Art of Self-Assurance — What Women Should Know," (Harper Business, 2014).

22. Katty Kay and Claire Shipman, "The Confidence Gap," *The Atlantic*, May 2014, http://www.theatlantic.com/magazine/archive/2014/05/the-confidence-gap/359815.

23. "First Aid For Common Confidence Emergencies," *Redbook,* June 2016, http://archive.org/stream/Redbook_June_2016_USA/Redbook_June_2016_USA_djvu.txt.

24. Valerie Young, "The Secret Thoughts of Successful Women: Why Capable People Suffer From the Imposter Syndrome, and How to Thrive In Spite of It," (Crown Business, 2011).

25. Rosabeth Moss Kanter, "Ten Reasons People Resist Change," *Harvard Business Review*, September 25, 2012, http://hbr.org/2012/09/ten-reasons-people-resist-chang.

26. Susan M. Heathfield, " What Makes Up Your Company Culture," *The Balance,* last modified April 1, 2018, http://www.thebalance.com/what-makes-up-your-company-culture-1918816.

27. William Arruda, "Nine Misconceptions About Personal Branding," *Forbes*, November 5, 2017, http://www.forbes.com/sites/williamarruda/2017/11/05/nine-misconceptions-about-personal-branding/#7c69d80b737a.

28. Robin Madell, "Does Gender Matter When It Comes to Your Mentor?" *The Glass Hammer*, March 28, 2012, http://theglasshammer.com/2012/03/28/does-gender-matter-when-it-comes-to-your-mentor/.

29. Jennifer Warner, "Dark Chocolate Takes Bite Out of Stress," WebMD, November 13, 2009, http://www.webmd.com/balance/stress management/news/20091113/dark-chocolate-takes-bite-out-of-stress.

30. Whitney Johnson, "The Toot-Your-Own-Horn Gender Bias," *Harvard Business Review*, June 8, 2010, http://hbr.org/2010/06/the-toot-your-own-horn-gender.

Made in the USA
Middletown, DE
09 June 2018